WOODCRAFT

THE CLASSIC, SUCCINCT GUIDE TO CAMP LIFE IN THE WOODS AND WILDS

BY **ELMER H. KREPS**

ORIGINALLY PUBLISHED IN 1919

LEGACY EDITION

THE LIBRARY OF AMERICAN OUTDOORS CLASSICS BOOK 10

FEATURING

REMASTERED CLASSIC WORKS OF THE HIGHEST

QUALITY FROM **THE TIMELESS MASTERS AND**

TEACHERS OF CAMPING, OUTDOORS SKILLS,

WOODCRAFT, AND TRADITIONAL HANDCRAFTS

Doublebit Press
Eugene. OR

INTRODUCTION

To The Doublebit Press Legacy Edition

Woodcraft by Elmer Kreps addresses many of the old-time tricks and ways of the woods that some of the more comprehensive instructional manuals of the day left out. Originally published in 1919, Kreps includes some of the less common, but enjoyable activities of the wilds. These included instruction on making camp furnishings and clothing, axemanship, camp fire building and its various uses, snowshoeing (and making your own snowshoes), food preparation and camp kitchens, building permanent camps and long-term shelter, horse packing, and traveling in the wild (or, the *bush*).

This text was one of the more popular volumes originally published by the A. R. Harding company at the turn of the 20th Century. The Harding company published high-selling little manuals for more niche outdoors activities, such as hunting, fur tanning, trapping, foraging, and backwoods travel. This contrasts with the more common general camping and outdoors manuals of the day, giving Harding books an air of expertise about the topics contained within each. This volume represents the best camping instruction manual in the Harding collection, alongside their *3001 Questions and Answers* (by Harding) and *Camp and Trail Methods* (also by Kreps).

Kreps also authored *Science of Trapping* and a short manual of outdoors skills called *Camp and Trail Methods* (this present book contains different, but equally useful material than *Camp and Trail Methods*).

About the Library of American Outdoors Classics

The old experts of the woods and mountains taught timeless principles and skills for decades. Through their books, the old experts offered rich descriptions of the outdoor world and encouraged learning through personal experiences in nature. Over the last 125 years, camping, outdoors recreation, and woods activities have substantially changed. Many things have gotten simpler as gear has improved, and life outside or on the trail now brings with it many of the same comforts enjoyed in town. In addition, some activities of the olden days are now no longer in vogue, or are even outright considered inappropriate or illegal, such as high-impact camping practices like chopping down live trees. However, despite many of the positive changes in outdoors methods that have occurred over the years, *there are many other skills and much knowledge that have been forgotten* from the golden era of American outdoors recreation.

By publishing the Library of American Outdoors Classics, it is our goal at Doublebit Press to do what we can to preserve and share the works from forgotten teachers that form the cornerstone of the history of the American outdoors. Through remastered reprint editions of timeless classics of outdoor recreation, perhaps we can regain some of this lost knowledge for future generations.

Because there were fewer options for finding outdoors gear in the early 1900's, experts in *"woodcraft"* skills (not to be confused with today's use of the word to mean woodworking or making things of wood) had to have a deep knowledge of the basic building blocks of outdoor living. This involved not only surviving in the outdoors, but to also have a comfortable and enjoyable time. As Nessmuk puts it in his book *Woodcraft,* "We do not go to the woods to rough it; we go to smooth it — we get it rough enough in town. But let us live the simple, natural life in the woods, and leave all frills behind." Nessmuk did not advocate for folks to go outside and have a terrible time. That would be contrary to the whole point of getting outside. Instead, he advocated for a "simpler" life by leaving some of the creature comforts of the city behind, but also entering the outdoors in a smart and practiced way that made the experience a much more satisfying vacation from home. The goal is to be comfortable so you can focus on having a good time outside and take in everything exposure to nature can offer. However, to be comfortable, one has to know the ins and outs of camping and outdoors life. Despite all the advances in campcraft and outdoors recreation, the old masters of the woods would all likely argue that this will only come from practicing the basics.

Because there was no market yet for specialty outdoors recreational gear (and thus, few outfitters), most outdoors gear came from military surplus piles or was custom made. As such, the old masters of woodcraft often made their own gear suited to their tastes. Through much experience in the woods and field, the great outdoors experts had to know why things worked the way they did by understanding the great web of cause and effect in nature. They had to learn from experience why certain gear worked better in different conditions or know how to solve problems off-the-cuff when things got hairy. They used the basic blocks of camping and outdoors knowledge to fine-tune their gear. They gained experience whenever they could and tried things different ways so they could gain mastery over the fundamentals and see challenges from many angles.

Today, much of the outdoor experience has been greatly simplified by neatly arranged campsites at public campgrounds and gear that has been meticulously improved and tested in both the lab and the field. Many modern conveniences are only a brief trek away, with many parks, campgrounds, and even forests having easy-access roads, convenience stores, and even cell phone signal. In some ways, it is much easier to camp and go outdoors today, and that is a good thing! We should not be miserable when we go outside — lovers of the outdoors know the essential restorative capability that the woods can have on the body, mind, and soul. Although things have gotten easier on us in the 21st Century when it comes to the outdoors, it certainly does not mean that we should forget the foundations of outdoors lore, though. All modern camping skills, outdoors equipment, and cool gizmos that make our lives easier are all founded on principles of the outdoors that the old masters knew well and taught to those who would listen.

Every woods master had their own curriculum or thought some things were more important than others. This includes the present author — certain things appear in this book that other masters leave out of theirs. The old masters also taught common things in slightly different ways or did things differently than others. That's what makes each of the experts different and worth reading. There's no universal way of doing something, especially now. Learning to go about something differently helps with mastery or learn a new skill altogether. Again, to use the metaphor from the above paragraphs, outdoors skills mastery consists of learning the basic building blocks of outdoors living, woods and nature lore, and the art of packing properly for trips. Each master goes about describing these building blocks differently or shows a different aspect of them.

Therefore, we have decided to publish this Legacy Edition in our Library of American Outdoors Classics series. This book is an important contribution to the early American recreational outdoors literature and has important historical and collector value toward preserving the American outdoors tradition. The knowledge it holds is an invaluable reference for practicing skills and hand craft methods. Its chapters thoroughly discuss some of the essential building blocks of knowledge that are fundamental but may have been forgotten as equipment gets fancier and technology gets smarter. In short, this book was chosen for Legacy Edition printing because much of the basic skills and knowledge it contains has been forgotten or put to the wayside in trade for more modern conveniences and methods.

Although the editors at Doublebit Press are thrilled to have comfortable experiences in the woods and love our high-tech and light-weight equipment, we are also realizing that the basic skills taught by the old masters are more essential than ever as our culture becomes more and more hooked on digital stuff. We don't want to risk forgetting the important steps, skills, or building blocks involved with thriving in the outdoors. The Legacy Edition series represents the essential contributions to the American outdoors tradition by the great experts of outdoors life and traditional hand crafting.

With technology playing a major role in everyday life, sometimes we need to take a step back in time to find those basic building blocks used for gaining mastery – the things that we have luckily not completely lost and has been recorded in books over the last two centuries. These skills aren't forgotten, they've just been shelved. *It's time to unshelve them once again and reclaim the lost knowledge of self-sufficiency.*

Based on this commitment to preserving our outdoors and handcraft heritage, we have taken great pride in publishing this book as a complete original work. We hope it is worthy of both study and collection by outdoors folk in the modern era of outdoors and traditional skills life.

Unlike many other photocopy reproductions of classic books that are common on the market, this Legacy Edition does not simply place poor photography of old texts on our pages and use error-prone optical scanning or computer-generated text. We want our work to speak for itself, and reflect the quality demanded by our customers who spend their hard-earned money. With this in mind, each Legacy Edition book that has been chosen for publication is carefully remastered from original print books, *with the Doublebit Legacy Edition printed and laid out in the exact way that it was presented at its original publication.* We provide a beautiful, memorable experience that is as true to the original text as best as possible, but with the aid of modern technology to make as beautiful a reading experience as possible for books that are typically over a century old.

Because of its age and because it is presented in its original form, the book may contain misspellings, inking errors, and other print blemishes that were common for the age. However, these are exactly the things that we feel give the book its character, which we preserved in this Legacy Edition. During digitization, we ensured that each illustration in the text was clean and sharp with the least amount of loss from being copied and digitized as possible.

Full-page plate illustrations are presented as they were found, often including the extra blank page that was often behind a plate. For the covers, we use the original cover design to give the book its original feel. We are sure you'll appreciate the fine touches and attention to detail that your Legacy Edition has to offer.

For outdoors enthusiasts who demand the best from their equipment, this Doublebit Press Legacy Edition reprint was made with you in mind. Both important and minor details have equally both been accounted for by our publishing staff, down to the cover, font, layout, and images. It is the goal of Doublebit Legacy Edition series to preserve outdoors heritage, but also be cherished as collectible pieces, worthy of collection in any outdoorsperson's library and that can be passed to future generations.

Every book selected to be in this series offers unique views and instruction on important skills, advice, tips, tidbits, anecdotes, stories, and experiences that will enrichen the repertoire of any person who enjoys escaping the city and finding their way to the trails of the wilds. To learn the most basic building blocks of outdoors life leads to mastery of all its aspects.

Studying This Book

The pages within this book present an overwhelming amount of information, facts, and directions to memorize that are often outdated and at the least, out of practice by modern standards. That doesn't mean that these pages have nothing to teach! It's just going to likely be new stuff for many readers.

Our one suggestion is *don't try to memorize everything,* especially when you're thumbing through the book or even reading it cover-to-cover. Writings from the late 1800's to early 1900's can be dense and out of style for someone not used to reading these types of books. Instead, gain some basic familiarity with each topic by thumbing through the pages, looking at the illustrations, and seeing the section headers. Then, choose a few topics or skills for deeper study.

Before camping or other outdoors trips can even begin, some planning and reflection is useful, which may be best done in town before you go out to the field. First, it might be helpful to read through the book with plans in mind. The book can provide useful material for close study and reflection when in town before you head out to the field to practice.

Secondly, once you've come up with a practice plan, you will of course want to start doing tasks and skills in the field. Doublebit Legacy books and the Library of American Outdoors Classics represents many field skills to master that have long sense been out of practice, but hopefully not forgotten! These include making and trying different kinds of tents or shelters, cooking (including any fish and game caught by you in the field), making many types of fires, setting up camp to suit your personal needs, beating the bugs and elements, understanding the terrain and weather, making furniture, brushing up on your nature lore, emergency survival, and testing your personal outfit and tools.

Any of the old tutors of woodcraft will tell you in their classic books that you can only truly learn how to go camping and do woodcraft by *actually doing it*. Home study indeed does you well by using the many guidebooks that have been published over the previous 125 years. However, hundreds more lessons will become immediately available to you the moment you start with some of the old-style tasks. This old style of outdoorsing is indeed outdated in many ways, but the approach still has much to teach modern campers who have become accustomed to carved out campsites, cabin and RV camping, and high-tech equipment.

Before the days of outfitters, outdoors adventurers made their gear, which was tailored to their individual needs. Many experiments were done in the field to tweak their gear to get that ever-changing point of "perfect." Aside from experiencing wonderful lessons in history, getting outside and doing some of the activities this book will give you an appreciation for modern advances in outdoors and handcraft method and tools of the trade, as well as a deeper understanding of the foundations of outdoors and hand-craft life in the event that your gear fails you or you otherwise find yourself in situations where knowing the principles will get you unstuck fast.

If we were to tally up each of the individual tips in the Doublebit Library of American Outdoors Classics, they would easily number in the thousands. The old masters represent centuries of previous knowledge that have been all but lost to 21st Century, technology-driven folks. To this point, although experience and *actually doing stuff* are the best forms of learning, taking a mindful approach to study of these works also benefit your development as a competent outdoorsperson and handcrafter.

You may also find it invaluable to take these volumes with you on your camping or other outdoors trips. In addition to having reading material on a variety of topics in the field for down time, you'll also find a thousand things to try in these pages if you're bored. Although skills may be best studied when in the field through experience and reflection, you may also study woods skills at home as well. Gaining familiarity through reading, videos, and other media are a great start toward building your ability toward gaining mastery in the field.

So, without blabbering on further, we hope you enjoy your Doublebit Legacy Edition. May your trails be clear and your experiences be memorable!

- The Doublebit Press Editors

WOODCRAFT

By E. H. KREPS

Published by

PELTRIES PUBLISHING CO.

Incorporated

71 W. 23d Street   -:-   New York

PREFACE.

Elmer H Kreps was born in Union county, Pa., in 1880. At that time large and small game of the various species common to Central Pennsylvana was plentiful in the neighborhood of his home. From his early boyhood he took a great interest in hunting and trapping. As he grew older he visited various parts of the United States and Canada, and being a keen observer, picked up a vast amount of information about life in the woods and fields.

Mr. Kreps has written many articles on various subjects connected with hunting and trapping and this little booklet is a collection of Woodcraft articles from his pen. Mr. Kreps is an accomplished artist as well as writer, and the illustrations in Woodcraft are reproduced from his sketches.

We feel sure that this collection of articles will prove of value to many men and boys who are interested in living in the woods and no one will be more happy than Mr Kreps if his work helps brighten the life of trappers and hunters, in whom he is always interested.

EDITOR FUR NEWS.

BUILDING THE HOME CAMP

The first camp I remember making, or remodeling, was an old lumber camp, one side of which I partitioned off and floored. It was clean and neat appearing, being made of boards, and was pleasant in warm weather, but it was cold in winter, so I put up an extra inside wall which I covered with building paper. Then I learned the value of a double wall, with an air space between, a sort of neutral ground where the warmth from the inside could meet the cold from without, and the two fight out their differences. In this camp I had a brick stove with a sheet iron top, and it worked like a charm.

But that was not really a wilderness camp, and while I realize that in many of the trapping districts where it is necessary to camp, there are often these deserted buildings to be found, those who trap or hunt in such places are not the ones who must solve the real problems of camp building. It is something altogether different when we get far into the deep, silent forest, where the sound of the axe has never yet been heard, and sawed lumber is as foreign as a linen napkin in a trapper's shack. But the timber is there, and the trapper has an ax and the skill and strength to use it, so nothing more is really needed. Let us suppose we are going to build a log cabin for a winter's trapping campaign. While an axe is the only tool necessary, when two persons work together, a narrow crosscut saw is a great labor-saver, and if it can be taken conveniently the trappers or camp builders will find that it will more than pay for the trouble. Other things very useful in this work are a hammer, an auger, a pocket measuring tape, and a few nails, large, medium and small sizes. Then to make a really pleasant camp a window of some kind must be provided, and for this purpose there is nothing equal to glass.

Right here a question pops up before us. We are going on this trip far back into the virgin forest, and the trail is long and rough; how then can we transport an unwieldy crosscut saw and such fragile stuff as glass? We will remove the handles from the saw and bind over the tooth edge a grooved strip of wood. This makes it safe to carry, and while still somewhat unhandy it is the best we can do, for we cannot shorten its length. For the window, we will take only the glass—six sheets of eight by ten or ten by fourteen size. Between each sheet we place a piece of corrugated packing board, and the whole is packed in a case, with more of the same material in top and bottom. This makes a package which may be handled almost the same as any other merchandise, and we can scarcely take into the woods anything that will give greater return in comfort and satisfaction.

If we are going to have a stove in this cabin we will also require a piece of tin or sheet iron about 18 inches square, to make a safe stovepipe hole, but are we going to have a stove or a fireplace? Let us consider this question now.

On first thought the fireplace seems the proper thing, for it can be constructed in the woods where the camp is made, but a fireplace so made may or may not be satisfactory. If we know the principles of proper fireplace construction we can make one that will not smoke the camp, will shed the proper amount of heat, and will not consume more fuel than a well-behaved fireplace should, but if one of these principles be violated, trouble is sure to result. Moreover, it is difficult to make a neat and satisfactory fireplace without a hammer for dressing the stones, and a tool of this kind will weigh as much as a sheet iron stove, therefore it is almost as difficult to take into the woods. Then there is one or two days' work, perhaps more, in making the fireplace and chimney, with the added uncertainty of its durability, for there are only a few kinds of stones that will stand heat indefinitely without cracking. On the other hand the fireplace renders the use of a lamp unnecessary, for it will throw out enough light for all ordinary needs.

The good points of the stove are that it can be made by anybody in a half day's time; it does not smoke the camp, does not black the cooking utensils, gives the maximum amount of heat from the minimum quantity of fuel, and will not give out or go bad unexpectedly in the middle of the winter. If you leave it to me our camp will be equipped with a sheet iron stove. While the stove itself is not now to be considered, we must know before we commence to build what form of heating and cooking apparatus will be installed.

Having decided on which part of the country is to be the centre of operations, we look for a suitable site for our cabin. We find it near a stream of clear water. Nearby is a stretch of burned land covered thinly with second growth saplings, and near the edge of the evergreen forest in which we will build our camp stands plenty of dead timber, tamarack, white spruce, and a few pine stubs, all of which will make excellent firewood. In the forest itself we find straight spruce trees, both large and small, balsam, and a few white birches, the loose bark of which

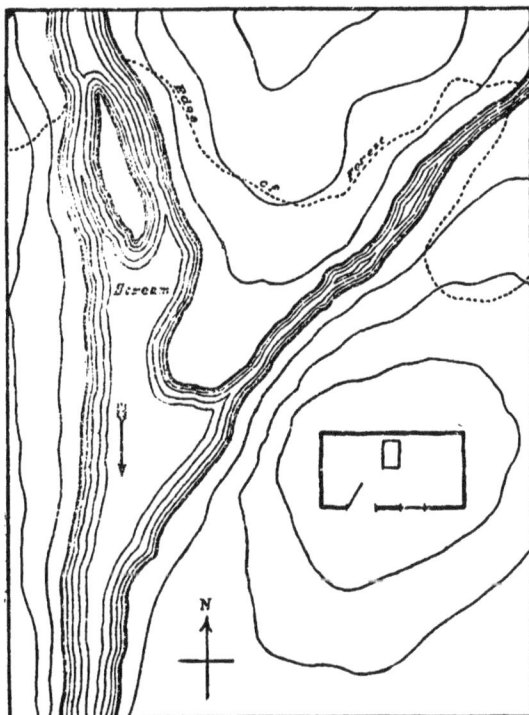

CHART SHOWING LOCATION OF CAMP.

will make the best kindling known. Within three rods of the stream and 50 yards from the burn is a rise of ground, high enough to be safe from the spring freshets, and of a gravelly ground which is firm and dry. This is the spot on which we will construct our cabin, for here we have good drainage, shelter from the storms, water and wood near at hand, and material for the construction of the camp right on the spot.

The first thing to settle is the size of the proposed building. Ten by fourteen feet, inside measurement, is a comfortable size for a home cabin for two men. If it were to be used merely as a stopping camp now and then it should be much smaller, for the small shack is easier warmed and easier to build. I have used

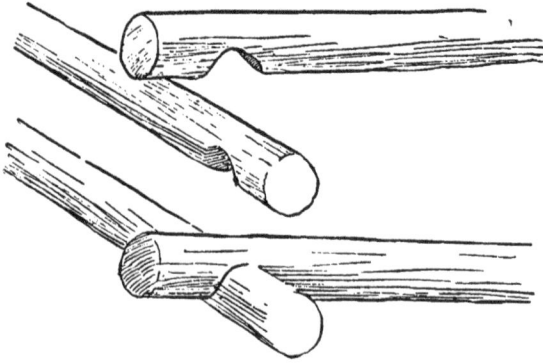

THE CORNER CONSTRUCTION.

camps for this purpose measuring only six and a half by eight feet, and found them plenty large for occasional use only. But this cabin is to be our headquarters, where we will store our supplies and spend the stormy days, so we will make it ten by fourteen feet. There is just one spot clear of trees where we can place a camp of this size, and we commence here felling trees from which to make logs for the walls. With the crosscut saw

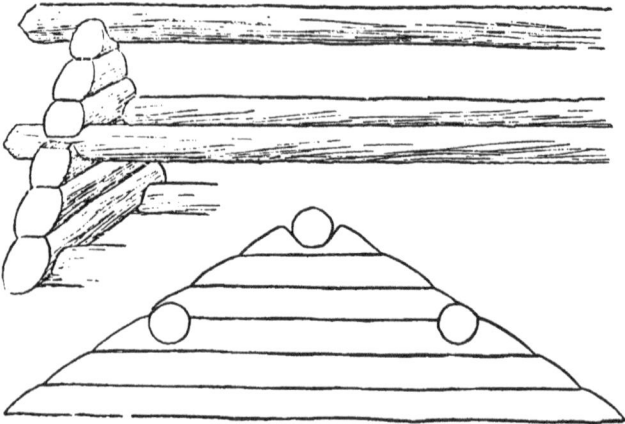

THE GABLES.

we can throw the straight spruce trees almost anywhere we want them, and we drop them in places which will be convenient and save much handling. As soon as a tree is cut we measure it off and saw it into logs. These must be cut thirteen and seventeen feet long, and as they will average a foot in diameter at the stump there will be an allowance of three feet for walls and over-lap, or 18 inches at each end. We cut the trees as near the ground as we can conveniently, and each tree makes two or three logs. All tall trees standing near the camp site must be cut, and used if possible, for there is always danger that a tree will blow over on the camp some time, if within reach.

On the spot chosen for the camp we now place two of the long logs, parallel with each other and exactly ten feet apart. We block them on the outside so they cannot be moved easily out of position. Then we place two of the short logs across the ends and in these we cut half-round notches directly over the places where they rest on the long logs, and almost half through each piece. After cutting these notches we turn the logs notched side down, and these cuts, if they have been properly done, fit snugly over the long logs, thus binding the four pieces together and forming the first round of the walls.

Before going farther now we must decide just where we are going to have the doorway of our cabin. We will place it on the south side, for we like to have the warm sunrays come in when the door is open, and if placed on the north or west sides it admits too much cold. We will place it near one end and then we can also put our window in the same side. About two or three feet from the corner we will cut out a section from the top of the log, making the cut four inches deep and two and a half feet wide, the bottom being hewn smooth and the ends sawed down square. Then we cut one of the balsam trees and saw a section from the butt the length of the proposed doorway. This should be not less than five feet, so we make it this length. Then we split through the centre with the axe and a pair of wooden wedges, and hew the two halves into two smooth planks. We also make a plank two and a half feet long. When these planks are finished we stand the two long ones upright in the place cut in the log and nail them firmly. We see that they stand perfectly plumb and in line with one another, then we nail the short plank across the top, thus completing our doorway. On this side, as the walls are laid up, we saw each log off squarely at the proper place and push it up against the door frame, fastening it there by nailing through the plank. The notches are cut to such a depth at the corners that the logs fit one against the other and this leaves no large cracks to close.

To make our cabin comfortable it must have a floor and we have this in mind as we work. Before building the wall higher we will lay our sills for the floor, for it is difficult to get these cut to the proper length and fitted in place after the walls are completed and the timber must be brought in through the doorway. We cut three straight logs about eight inches thick in the middle and 14 feet long. These are bedded into the ground in the cabin, one along each side wall and the other in the centre. They must be placed at an even height and this is determined by means of a straight ten-foot pole, which when placed across these logs should rest on each. If one of them is too high in spots we dress these places down with the axe.

We will now leave the floors and proceed with building the walls. Round by round the logs are notched and fitted into place, until the walls have reached a height of about four feet. Then we make a window boxing of planks and fasten it in the wall in the same way we did the door frame. The ends of the logs are butted against the window frame and fastened with large nails, driven through the planks into the logs. But before making the window frame the size of the proposed window must be determined, and this is done by measuring the width of the glass and making the proper allowance for the sash. When the logs

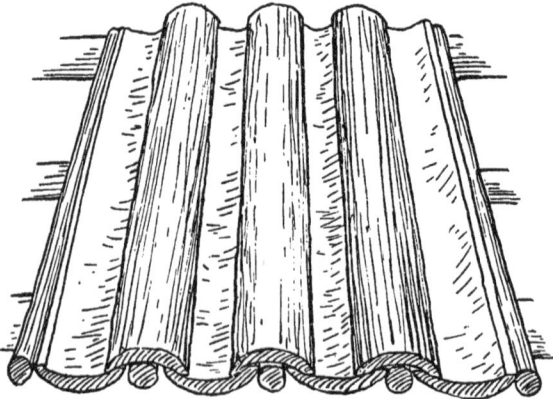

THE ROOF.

are placed in the walls we try to select timbers of such a size that one round of logs will come within about three inches of the top of the window boxing, and the next log is cut out to fit down over this window and the frame is nailed fast to this log. The same thing is done when the top of the door frame is reached, and this gives a greater degree of rigidity to the walls.

When the walls have been raised to a height of about six and a half feet above the floor sills we commence work on the gables. These are constructed by placing a full length log across the end, a shorter one on top of this, continuing thus until high enough. This is best done by setting a pole up in the end of the camp exactly in the middle of the end wall, the top being just the height of the proposed gable. From the top of this straight pole, poles are run down to each corner and these give the slope of the gables, also of the roof. The logs are then cut off on an incline at the ends to conform with the line of this pole, and are fastened one on top of another by boring holes and driving wooden pins into them. When both gables have been raised to half their height we cut two 17-foot binding poles, each six inches thick in the middle, and notch them into the logs of the gables. These logs or poles not only give more stability to the gables, but they also make a support for the roof, and are a nice foundation for a loft on which to store articles after the camp is finished. When the ends are brought up to within about eight inches of the required height a stout, straight ridge pole of the same length as the binding poles is placed on top, and notched lightly into the top log.

Our camp is now ready for the roof, and what are we to use for this most important part I have no doubt that camp roofs have caused more gray hairs for woodsmen than any of the other problems they have to solve. If it were early summer when the bark could be peeled from cedar and spruce trees we would have no trouble, but bark is not available now. About the only style of roof that we can make now is what is called a scoop roof, made from split logs. We must find a straight-grained, free-splitting wood for this, and of the woods at hand we find balsam the best, so we cut balsam trees about eight or ten inches in diameter, and make logs from the butt of each, about seven feet long, so that they will reach from the top of the ridge-pole to the walls and extend a foot beyond. These we split through the centre and hollow out each in a trough form, by cutting notches in the flat side, without cutting the edges, and splitting out the sections between. We place a layer of these the entire length of the roof, hollow side up, and notch each in place so that it cannot slip or rock. Between each set of these troughs we will place a three-inch pole, and on top of the pole we place marsh moss. Then we place over these poles a second layer of the troughs, hollow side down, and over the ridge pole we place a large, full-length trough. This latter we must make by hewing a log flat on one side and then hollowing it out, for we cannot find a tree with such a straight grain that we can split a 17-foot length without more or less of a twist.

Before completing our roof, in fact when the first layer of scoops are placed on, we must make provision for our stove pipe, for it must have an outlet through the roof, and the location the stove is to have in the cabin must be determined. A hole 12 or 14 inches square is left in the roof, by using a few short scoops, and this hole is covered with the sheet of tin we brought for the purpose, and a slightly oblong hole is cut in this for the stove pipe. The edge of this hole we turn up with the hammer, which makes it waterproof, and when finished it is such a size that the pipe makes a snug fit. The whole thing is so arranged that water cannot run under from the top, but this is difficult to explain.

A roof like this causes a lot of work, in fact as much as the remainder of the camp in some cases, but if carefully made it is a good roof, warm and waterproof. It must be well mossed or snow will sift in, and the lower ends of the troughs, from where they cross the walls, should be cut deeper than the portion above. If this is not done the ice which forms in the ends of these troughs will back the water up until it runs over the edges and down the walls of the cabin. It may even be necessary occasionally during the winter to clean the snow off the lower edge of the roof and clip the ice from the troughs with a hatchet. The steeper the roof the less trouble there will be from this source.

With the roof completed our cabin becomes a real shelter and we can camp inside at night. If necessary the flooring may be postponed for a few days, but we may as well finish it at once, so we clean out the chips and commence laying the floor. This we make of straight spruce poles about four or five inches thick. In the end of the camp where our beds are to be we leave them in their natural round state, merely flattening them on the underside where they rest on the sills, to make them fit and lie firmly in their places. But when the floor has grown at this end to a width of about four feet we adopt a different plan. We now hew the poles straight and smooth on one side their entire length, and

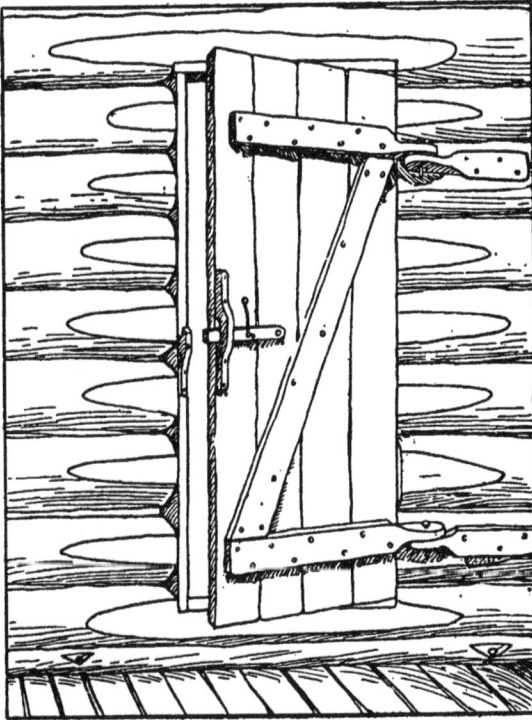

THE DOOR.

flatten the underside where they rest on the sills, also straighten the sides so they fit up snugly against one another. At the place where the stove is to be placed we leave an opening of two and a half by four feet, and around this place we fasten smooth pieces of wood about four inches thick, so that it makes of the opening a sort of box. When our floor is completed we nail down along each wall, a pole, which covers the ends of the floor poles and holds them all firmly in place.

To complete our cabin now we need only a door, a window, and something to close the cracks. For a door we split cedar or balsam wood into planks, which we place on edge in notches cut in a log, and hew down smoothly on both sides with the axe.

Then we straighten the edges and measuring our door frame carefully we fit the boards into the opening, binding them all together by nailing across near each end a narrow board. We also place a strip diagonally across the door from near one corner to the opposite, to stiffen the door and prevent warping. Hinges we make of wood, fasten them together with a single large nail through each, and fasten the door to the wall. Then on the outside we hew the ends of the logs until they are flush with the edges of the door frame, and nail a flattened strip along both sides of the doorway. This is not absolutely necessary, but it gives the doorway a more finished appearance, and increases the rigidity of the wall.

Our window sash also makes considerable work. For this we split soft, dead cedar and hew it into three-inch strips. From these we make a frame that will fit inside the window boxing, and make the strips of this frame flush at the corners by cutting away half of each. Then at the proper places we fit our lighter cross strips, sinking them into the wood at the ends, and fastening with small nails. Grooves are then cut in the strips and the frame itself to receive the sheets of glass, which are put in place and fastened with tacks. The window is then placed in the wall and secured by nailing narrow strips of wood against it. As a window at its best is apt to admit a lot of cold air it will pay well to spend some time at this work and make the window fit snugly.

All that now remains to be done is to close the cracks between the logs. Since our logs were of a uniform size and have been well notched down there are no large cracks, and no blocking is needed. The warmest chinking, outside of rags, which we do not have, is woods moss. That found growing on rocks and logs is best, for it does not dry out and shrink as much as marsh moss, and there is an abundance of this near at hand. We gather a few bags of this moss and with a piece of wood we drive it into the cracks all around the walls. We also keep a small quantity of this moss in the cabin, for no matter how firmly it is driven into the cracks it will shrink and become loose after awhile, and this must be tightened and more moss driven in.

Our little cabin is now complete. It has taken much hard work to build it, but it is worth the effort for it is a comfortable, home-like camp. The cold winter winds may howl through the forest and the snow may fall to a depth of several feet, but here we can live as comfortably as woodsmen can expect to live in the wilds.

FURNISHING THE HOME CAMP

A single day's work will do wonders towards making a cabin comfortable. Sometimes through press of more important work, such as getting out a line of traps while the season is yet young, the trapper may well neglect these touches of comfort, and the simplest of camp furnishings will answer until a stormy day keeps him indoors, when he can make good use of his time in making camp furniture. A bed and a stove or fireplace are the only absolutely necessary furnishings to start with, if other work demands immediate attention.

But in our own case such neglect is not at all necessary. The preceding chapter saw our cabin completed, that is the walls, roof and floor, all that can really be called cabin, but much more work will be required before it is really comfortable and ready for occupancy. Providing the camp with suitable furniture and adding conveniences and comfort is the next step, so while we have time and there is nothing to hinder the work we will push it along.

Most important of all camp furnishings is the stove. Nothing else adds so much to the cheerfulness and home-like aspect of a camp as a properly enclosed, well behaved fire, which warms up the room, enables us to cook our food indoors, and dispenses the gloom of night by driving the darkness into the farthest corners. If the weather is cold nothing in the camp is so indispensable.

For the lodge which we built in the preceding chapter we will make a stove of sheet iron. I have made a number of camp stoves by riveting together four sections of new, unbent stovepipe into a square sheet, bending this into proper shape, fitting ends, and cutting holes for cooking utensils and for the pipe. But for this camp we have secured from a hardware store a pipe of sheet iron three feet wide by four feet long. We now place this on the floor of the cabin and measure off from each end 17 inches, then on each edge at the 17-inch mark we make a three-inch cut. This we do by holding the sheet metal on a block or flat topped stump, placing the corner of the axe on the metal at the proper place, and striking on the head with a billet of wood. Then we place a straight edged strip of wood across the end on the 17-inch mark, and standing on this wood we pull the end of the metal upward, bending it to a right angle. The other end is treated the same way and this leaves the metal in the form of a box, three feet long, 17 inches high, and 14 inches wide, open on top and at both ends. Now we turn this upside down and in the top we cut two seven-inch holes, as round as we can make them. These are to hold the cooking utensils. Near one end we cut a small hole, not more than three and a half inches in diameter. The edge of this hole we cut at intervals all the way around, making straight, one-half inch cuts. Then we turn these edges up, and we have a stove-pipe hole, with a collar to hold the pipe in place. We now close the rear end of the stove by bending three inches of the sides into a right angle, the same amount of the top being bent down. This is the purpose of the three-inch cuts we made when we first commenced the work. Now we rivet a piece of sheet-iron into this end, using for rivets the head ends of wire nails. They must be cut short and riveted on the head of an axe. Beneath the top of the stove, between the cooking holes we rivet a folded strip of metal; this is to stiffen th top. Then we turn in three inches of the front of the stove and rivet the corners where they lap. This leaves an eight-inch opening in front over which we will hinge a door. This door must have some kind of fastening, and a simple little twist of wire working in a punch hole is easily arranged and convenient. We can make a very crude stove of this if we like, but we do not want that kind, so we take plenty of time and turn out a satisfactory article.

Our stove is now completed except for the covers which are easily made. We set it up in the box-shaped opening left in the floor and fill around it with sand to a height of six inches, also fill the inside to that height. While doing this we must see that the stove stands perfectly level, and that the pipe hole is directly beneath the hole in the roof. This makes a fireproof stove and the bed of sand holds it rigidly in place. A draft is made beneath the door by scraping away a little sand. The pipe is five-inch size and we fit it with a damper for that is the way to regulate the draft and keep the heat from going up the pipe.

Our stove completed and in working order we next turn our attention to the bed, since it ranks second in importance. We set an upright post four inches thick and three feet long against the sidewall about five feet from the end of the room and nail it firmly in position. Then at a height of about two feet from the floor we fasten to the wall another four-inch piece, this extending in a horizontal position from the post to the end wall. Then we set up a corner post at the foot of the bed, plac-

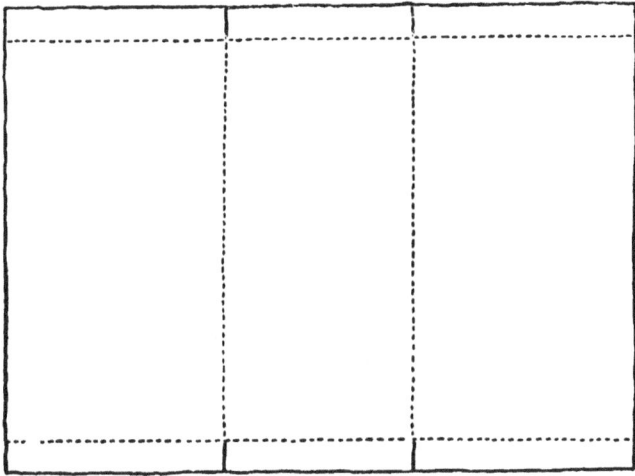

1

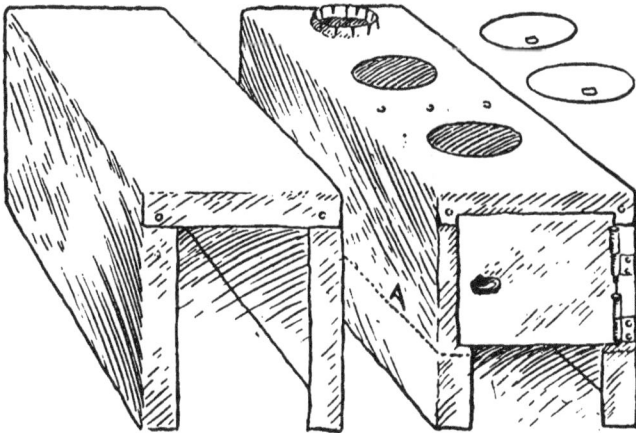

2   3

THE STOVE. 1. BEFORE BENDING. 2. AFTER BENDING.
3. STOVE COMPLETE. STAND IN SAND TO LINE A.

ing it five feet from the end wall and nailing the top securely to
the roof binding pole. In line with this against the end wall we
set up another three-foot post and spike it solidly to the logs of
the wall. Then we cut notches in these two latter posts two
feet above the floor and into this we fit and nail fast a four-inch
cross strip. We now have the foundation for our bed and we
make the bottom of straight, smooth poles, nailed fast to the
horizontal ends. These poles must all be of about the same
thickness to make a satisfactory bed, otherwise some of them
will bend or spring while the stiff ones will not. If it were summer now we would line this bunk with bark to keep the
balsam needles from falling through, but since we cannot get
bark at this time of year we cannot do this. We make the side
and end of the bed by nailing poles against the posts. Then we
fill the bed with balsam boughs. These are the ends of the
branches and the heaviest stems are less than a fourth-inch thick.
We commence at the head and stand the boughs on end at an
angle, stems down. When entirely filled we have a soft and
fairly comfortable bed, of course not equal to the spring bed we
have at home, but then we are not expecting home comforts in
the big woods, and we are always tired enough to rest well in
a bough bed. For pillows we use grain bags in which we place
our extra clothing.

This bed is at its best when freshly filled. Each night's
use reduces its softness, and the comfort decreases at a like
rate. The only way to keep a bough bed in good condition is
to replace the bough filling occasionally with fresh evergreens.
When we kill some big game animal, a deer or caribou, we will
dry the skin and place it on our bed, hair side up, for this will
make the bed warmer and softer.

The table is next in order. Many trappers think a table too
much of a luxury and accordingly dispense with it, but a home
camp is far from complete without it and it is an easy piece of
furniture to make. It should be placed on the south side of the
cabin before the window, so that we can get the advantage of
the light. We will stand up two posts of the proper height
about two feet from the wall and six feet apart. These we secure
in place by nailing them to the floor. From the tops of these
posts to the wall we place flattened pieces of wood and secure
them by nailing to the wall and to the posts. This is the foundation or framework for our table. The top we will make of three
straight eight-inch logs hewn on one side to the center, and

CAMP FURNITURE. TABLE, BENCH AND LAMP SHELF.

flattened on the other side at the ends. When placed on the supports, flat side up, and fastened by nailing at the ends, we have the table completed. It is rough, but it answers our purpose as well as a more finished one.

In front of the table we will place a bench. This we will make from a hewn log, half round, and in the round side near each end we bore holes for the legs. These are bored at such an angle that the legs will stand about 20 inches apart at the base. The legs are made of two-inch sticks whittled to fit the holes and driven in, the lower ends being cut off afterwards at the proper length to make the bench stand firmly, and at the right height. We will also make another shorter bench which we will place by the side of the stove. Perhaps when a stormy day comes we will make a couple of chairs, but for the present at least these two benches will serve very well.

We cannot be long in the woods until we realize the need of some means of securing our food where it will be inaccessible to woods mice. These little creatures are a serious pest and can soon ruin a bag of flour or a side of bacon if they are able to get at it. In an effort to place my flour where they could not reach it I suspended it from the ridgepole with a piece of codfish line, but the nimble mice went up and down that cord like monkeys. Then I made a platform and suspended it from the roof with four pieces of hay baling wire. On this I placed my food; but even here I found it was not safe, for the mice dropped onto the platform from the roof poles. The only way I found that was perfectly satisfactory was to make a tight box with a well fitted cover in which to keep the food supply. As a result I made a food box for each camp.

We have now found that it is necessary to have some means of preserving our food from the ravages of mice, and profiting by experience we do not waste our time on theories, but set to work to make a tight wooden box. If it were a time of the year when bark would peel we would make a frame of poles and cover it with bark. But this is impossible now, so we split boards from balsam and cedar and hew them flat and smooth. For the ends we make these boards two feet long and fasten them together by nailing strips across the ends of the boards after they have been placed side by side with the edges fitting one against another. The boards for the bottom and sides are made three feet long and these we nail to the ends. The cover is fitted to the top, but is not fastened.

Luxuries become necessities through use. The furnishings which we have so far brought into our cabin may be considered as coming properly under the heading of necessities. But there are many little extra pieces that may be added which may be called luxuries at first, but through use they become almost indispensable. On the walls we will build shelves and we find them very useful places for storing odds and ends. A small shelf is placed on the wall near the stove to hold the lamp, and another similar shelf for the same purpose is placed above the left end of the table. Then there are two or three longer shelves placed in convenient locations. These shelves are all made of hewn boards supported by stout pins driven into auger holes.

If we are not by this time too tired of making boards with an axe, we will make a wooden tub in which to wash our clothes. Since we have a saw this is not as difficult as it first appears. It is made square with sloping sides. The boards must be carefully fitted and securely nailed. Then, after we have made it as tight as possible by nailing we will gather a small quantity of spruce gum and run it into the cracks from the inside by means of a hot iron, in much the same way that we would solder tin plate. A wash basin can be made in the same way, but we have a tin basin in our outfit so we'll not need to make one.

Behind the stove we nail a slender pole, horizontally, onto wooden pins driven into auger holes, so that the pole is parallel with the wall and about six or eight inches from it. On this pole we place our socks and mitts to dry when we come in from the day's tramp. We hang our coats on nails driven into the wall. Our snowshoes we suspend from the roof with snare wire in the coolest part of the camp, so that the mice cannot eat the filling or the heat make it brittle.

Perhaps you would be interested in our camp outfit, for it is adapted to use in a camp of this kind. We have come into the woods for the fall and winter, and while we will go out occasionally for supplies of food, our outfit is supposed to be complete, and in it are all the articles needed for an entire winter's stay in the wilds. The following are the articles which we have brought with us as camp outfit: Two rabbit skin blankets, two large all-wool blankets, one large and one medium enameled kettle, two tea pails, one water pail, one large frying pan and two small ones, with sockets for handles, three enameled plates, two enameled cups, two table knives, two forks, two table spoons, two tea spoons, one reflecting baker, one wash basin, one small mirror, four towels, one alarm clock, one small oil lamp (bottom portion of a railroad lantern), three small axes with long handles, one cross-cut saw, one hand saw, two flat files, two sharpening stones (pocket size), one auger, one hammer, assorted nails, a dozen small bags for holding food, a small box of medicines, and a repair kit, consisting of needles, thread, wax, scissors, awl and small pliers.

The above is the actual camp outfit and does not include personal belongings, such as guns, traps, toilet articles, compasses, clothing, snowshoes, etc., things which are used more on the trail than in camp, and while necessary in our business cannot rightfully be considered a part of the camp equipment. Even some of the articles mentioned, for instance the two small frying pans, are more for use on the trail than in the home cabin.

This, and the preceding chapter, describe what to my mind is an ideal camp for two persons and a perfect equipment for same. The camp site described could not be improved upon, and it is seldom that we find all of the requirements in any one place, yet the description is that of one of my own camp sites, and except for the size of camp and a few details of furnishings and outfit, also describes one of my cabins, one which I constructed and used while trapping in Canada.

OUTDOOR FOODS

That foods for outdoor men should differ from those eaten by people who work indoors may appear strange to some of us, but it is a fact that foods of the same class are not, as a rule, practical for both outdoor and indoor consumption. The requirements of people who work in the open air differ but little from those of the indoor workers, but it is mainly the source of supply that necessitates a different class of foods.

The indoor man lives in the midst of plenty. Almost anything his appetite demands he may have. The telephone makes it unnecessary for him to go to the store to place his order and the delivery man brings the goods to his back door. His better half, or perhaps a hired cook, prepares the food for him and he need not even worry about the time required for cooking or the work necessary to prepare and place the viands before him.

But with the outdoor man, by which I mean woodsman and others who are employed outdoors and do their own cooking far from a base of supplies, the conditions are altogether different. Perhaps the outer has carried his food a long distance on his back, or it may have been brought to his camp in a boat or canoe, or by team over a long and rough road, or even packed on horseback from 50 to 100 miles into the rough mountains. In either case it was necessary for him to select foods having certain qualities. In order to keep the bulk and weight down to a reasonable level all bulky, heavy, watery foods had to be eliminated. Such foods as would freeze in cold weather, decay, become rancid, or otherwise spoil if kept a long time without special care, had to be kept out of the list. Also such articles as do not contain much nutriment must be avoided, as well as those which are apt to prove harmful when used regularly. Not only that, but the entire outfit of food must be "well balanced," that is, it must have about the right proportions of the various food elements required by the human body. Too much salt pork and other preserved foods, with too little fresh food, may cause scurvy; various articles which are known to be difficult of digestion may cause chronic dyspepsia, while many constipating foods may in a different way lead to the same trouble. In addition nothing should be taken which is difficult to transport or apt to get broken and cause trouble while en route.

To sum it all up, the requirements in outdoor foods that are to be taken some distance to camp are as follows: First, reasonably light weight and small bulk; second, good keeping qualities; third, a high per cent. of nutrition; fourth, balance and total absence of injurious properties; fifth, adaptability to packing and transportation requirements. We might add to this the quality of being quickly and easily prepared, for, while this is not required in all of the food, it is necessary for all outdoor men to have a number of articles which may be prepared on short notice.

Breakfast in the woods is usually an early meal, in winter being invariably eaten before daylight, and this requires either quickly prepared foods or very early rising. Often, too, the woodsman comes in from a tramp long after dark. He has had a long, hard journey, perhaps having had only a lunch since daybreak, maybe not even that, and the cold, along with the exertion, has given him a marvelous appetite. On such occasions every minute that can be gained in cooking a nourishing meal is that much to the good. But short-order meals are not the thing for regular fare, for in time they will ruin any stomach.

Considering the first requisite, light weight and little bulk, we may include in our list as meeting these requirements, all kinds of dried fruits, vegetables, and meats, tea, coffee and condensed foods. Fresh vegetables and fruits are excluded from the list, for they are heavy and bulky and fail also in the second requirement, for they freeze easily in cold weather and sometimes do not keep well when it is warm. To make up for the lack of fresh fruits and vegetables we must take plenty of the dry kind, and it is also a good plan to have in the outfit a bottle of vinegar or fruit juice—lime juice is an excellent tonic or use in the woods and is a sure preventative of scurvy. Vegetables and fruit in tin or glass are also prohibitive except in a small way, as, for instance, the fruit juice, vinegar, pickles and condensed milk, all of which may be taken in small quantities. In general, however, canned goods should be avoided unless the trip is made by wagon or other means that does not prohibit taking heavy goods, in which case a quantity of food in tins may be taken. Eggs and other ultra-perishable goods are strictly prohibited. The taking of eggs and food in glass also violates requisite number five, for all such articles require far more care in handling than is practical on the bush trail.

Not only does the woodsman have to consider cooking and eating in camp but he must think as well of the many days that he will spend on the trail and there his food must be of the most condensed, light, nutritious and otherwise perfect form. He must therefore take with him to his home camp sufficient of this quality of food to fill his needs when he makes his long trips away from camp over the trap line or elsewhere, but always carrying with him his equipment and food for the trip.

A man can depend to some extent on game and fish, but if he is going far back into the wilderness where he cannot retreat in a day or two to civilization and a source of food supply he should be very sure that the game and fish are actually found in the place where he is going, that such game and fish will be available at all seasons, and that there will be no uncommon difficulty in securing it. Some kinds of big game animals migrate periodically or spasmodically; fish are sometimes hard to find in winter, and the hunting equipment may for one reason or another go wrong. For instance, the capsizing of a canoe may mean the loss of the only gun or all the ammunition in the party, and even a broken gun mainspring may cause great hardship. Of course a resourceful and expert woodsman would not starve even if turned adrift in the forest without food or gun, but few care to make the experiment or to risk going hungry. Therefore I advise taking enough food, so that it will not be necessary to depend on game. If there is game to be had it should, of course, be secured, for fresh meat is a great relief from the everlasting bacon and bannock and it tends to neutralize the constipating properties of such food. It is possible for one to live indefinitely on fresh meat and fish alone if forced to it; but the civilized appetite does not accept gracefully any such radical departures from what has now become the natural line of food. Moreover, the man who elects to live on game and fish alone must of necessity go hungry for long periods, in fact may be forced to face starvation when game is scarce and for one reason or another difficult to secure. Therefore the woodsman should not attempt to live wholly on fresh meat or to make so much allowance for game that he will suffer from hunger if the game is not procurable. No such sacrifice should be made merely to reduce the weight of the outfit.

Coming now to the matter of keeping qualities we find that any of the evaporated, dried or condensed foods on the market meet all requirements. Bacon, cured for winter use, may not remain in a perfectly sweet condition, and it is well to make sure before purchasing that the meat is well salted and smoked. Butter may become strong unless the weather is cold, but I have found that first-class creamery butter will keep nicely for a period of two and a half months in fairly cold weather. For a longer trip canned butter should be procured. It may be purchased in Canada from almost any grocer located in an outfitting point. While potatoes and other fresh vegetables are prohibited because of weight and bulk they are also eliminated from the list because they freeze in cold weather. A trapper must often be away from camp for a period of time varying from a few days to a week or more and anything that can freeze will surely do so in one night of "40 below" weather. As an exception to this rule I advise taking a few onions, for in spite of their weight they are a food worth considering. They freeze as readily as potatoes, but if they are kept frozen until time for use it will not hurt them in the least. There are many dishes that are greatly improved by an onion flavor and I am very fond of this evil-smelling vegetable when sliced and fried with steak. Ordinary canned goods containing water are tabooed in cold weather, for they freeze and burst the cans, besides falling short in the first requirement of camp foods, namely, light weight.

Nutrition in foods is a quality which needs but little expenditure of gray matter if one does not attempt to live a long period on an unvaried line. By taking a variety of foods and changing the menu frequently danger from lack of nutriment is reduced to the minimum. Condensed and dried foods are invariably very nutritious. With fresh meat occasionally the foods which I recommend will meet all requirements in this particular.

What has been said on the subject of nutrition in camp foods will suffice for the fourth requisite—perfect balance and lack of injurious elements. While I would not advise the use of one or two articles of food as a steady diet the kind I name in the lists given herewith, if used in the proportions given and a little fresh meat or fish can be sandwiched in here and there, no bad results will follow. On the other hand, if any of the articles, or especially a line of articles like the dried fruits, are omitted, I would not be responsible for the good health of the user.

Within the borders of civilization, and especially with those people doing office work or following any indoor occupation which does not require plenty of bodily exertion, constipation is a serious menace, in fact I think it is the cause of many ills which are generally attributed to other sources. In the woods it is somewhat different, for the long tramps and other violent exercises tend to keep the bowels open, but it is not so with all men, and especially with those who hail from the city. Even the seasoned woodsman should not trifle with anything of so serious a nature, for even to him chronic constipation may come as the result of a steady diet of white flour and other constipating foods. In the lists which I give the foods most harmful in this way are wheat flour, especially when used in baking powder bread, cheese, rice, beans and peas. The foods most valuable for offsetting the bad effects of the above are the dried fruits, especially prunes, and cornmeal. Fresh meat and onions act as laxatives also, but too much of any of these foods may cause the system to fortify itself against them and their good effects are reduced greatly. Many kinds of food are difficult to digest; but it should be remembered that all stomachs are not alike and what is indigestible for one man is easily assimilated by another. The only way to learn what foods are harmful and which ones are not is by trying them, but this should be done and the results known before going into the woods.

Tea and coffee are used extensively in the woods because they are very refreshing to tired travelers. Tea is especially invigorating. But both of these drinks, if used in excess, are harmful. Coffee injures the nervous system directly, while indirectly it works on other organs, and tea is injurious to the stomach, also the nerves. Taken in reasonable amount these drinks will do no harm, but they should never be used to the exclusion of water. The latter is the natural drink and we cannot use too much.

The fifth requirement in camp foods is one that must not be forgotten. On a long trip into the bush the outfit is sure to get a certain amount of rough usage; a pack strap may give way or the packer may stumble or slip and down goes the pack. With but few exceptions, then, everything which will not stand a reasonable amount of rough handling has no right to a place on the outer's list. The exceptions are a few articles which when taken in small quantities must be put up in glass and these few foods are pickles, vinegar and others of similar nature. If any other less breakable container can be found for these it is better to use it, but if these foods are in bottle same must be carefully packed to prevent breakage. Eggs are the most unsatisfactory of all foods for transportation into the wilds, for they are easily broken, cannot be kept during cold weather and spoil quickly when the weather is mild.

This is not an article on packing or otherwise transporting outfits into the bush, but I wish to say this in regard to packing foods, that all packages and containers should be as light as possible consistent with strength and durability. Paper sacks are not the proper thing, for they are so easily torn. It is by far the better plan to have small duck or muslin bags for all dry foods. Nothing should be taken if put up in wooden boxes or other containers having sharp edges or corners, but all such articles should be removed and placed in the cloth sacks. If this is impossible it is better to eliminate such goods from the list.

To give a list of foods which are suitable for steady diet in the wilds is easy, and it may be a perfect list, well balanced, nourishing and having all the other desirable qualities, yet it may not be satisfactory for general use. Individual tastes do not all follow the same channels and there are no end of people who could pick from any list of foods that I might give a number of articles which they cannot eat or which are not received kindly by their respective systems. Another thing is the difference in quantity of food consumed by different men. While a life in the open air with continuous physical exercise from before daylight until after dark develops an appetite in any man, with some men their appetites seem absolutely insatiable and they consume enormous quantities of food. It is therefore difficult to give a list which may be taken as an accurate guide and approximate quantities only can be given, these being in the present instance based on what I consider a normal woodsman's appetite. I give in the following lists quantities intended for one man for a month's use and if the lists look good they may be used as a basis on which to figure the amounts of food required for any length of time.

List No. 1.—Twenty pounds wheat flour and ten pounds cornmeal, or 25 pounds wheat flour and five pounds cornmeal; one and a half pounds best baking powder, free of alum; three pounds table salt (this is more than necessary for food, but allows for preserving game); ten pounds bacon or five pounds bacon and five pounds salt pork; one pound lard or "Crisco" (this is seldom needed if all bacon grease is saved and used for cooking); three pounds creamery or canned butter; 10 pounds beans, small or large, as preferred; four pounds split peas; five pounds evaporated fruit, either apples, apricots or peaches, assorted if desired; four pounds prunes; six pounds sugar (seven pounds if used in tea and coffee); two pounds tea (black, green or mixed) or three pounds ground coffee in airtight tins; one bottle, about two pounds, sour pickles; four pounds evaporated, unsweetened milk in small size tins; two pounds cheese; one ounce black pepper. Eighty-seven and a half to 89½ pounds total weight.

The foregoing is my standard list on which I have based many a purchase of supplies, and while I vary quantities sometimes, and add luxuries now and then, the list alone, just as given, makes an excellent one for real woods trips.

In the following I have cut down the quantities of some articles and added the equivalent in other goods, thus giving greater variety and making a ration that is less apt to grow tiresome in time.

List No. 2.—Eighteen pounds wheat flour and five pounds cornmeal; two pounds crackers or soda biscuits; one pound of best baking powder; three pounds table salt; six pounds bacon and four pounds salt pork; three and a half pounds creamery or canned butter; seven pounds beans; three pounds split peas; five pounds evaporated fruits, assorted as desired; four pounds prunes; eight pounds sugar; two pounds tea or three pounds coffee, ground and in airtight tins; two-pound bottle sour pickles; five pounds evaporated milk in small tins; four pounds rice; one pound seeded raisins; two ounces cinnamon; one ounce black pepper; two pounds cheese; five pounds Bermuda onions. Ninety and a half pounds to 91½ pounds total weight.

I think the above list will be more generally satisfactory than the first, but if the camper has preferences in regard to the kind of food selected he may use these lists only as a basis on which to figure. The weights given are net and do not include extra containers. It will be noted that the total weight is nearly the same in both; but the second allows for a more varied menu. I have added to this one four pounds of rice. The raisins, with the additional sugar and milk, are mainly for this dish. I have also added an extra half-pound of butter, for it will be needed to make rice pudding. The cinnamon is for use in apple sauce and on rice. By eliminating the crackers and half the salt a couple of pounds of oatmeal and a brick of maple sugar may be added, thereby again increasing the number of items without additional weight and making a good wholesome breakfast dish (oatmeal porridge), or one that can be prepared quickly, also providing syrup for the pancakes—"white hopes," as one of my camping companions called them.

Some of the above-named foods can be cooked satisfactorily only in the permanent camp, while others are suitable for use in camp or on the trail. When making long tramps away from my cabin and camping out at night by the side of a fire I like to travel as lightly equipped as possible without sacrificing comfort, therefore I carry very little camp equipment and especially few cooking utensils. This necessitates the use of very simple, easily prepared dishes. Ordinarily I carry only the following foods: Flour mixed with the proper amount of baking powder and salt; bacon, sliced and with the rind removed; oatmeal, sugar, butter, tea, and a small sack containing a few ounces of salt. The latter is for use in cooking game killed during the day. It will be obvious then that if the camper follows my plan he must base his quantities of these articles on the proportion of time which he believes will be spent on the trail or camping out. If the time so spent will be limited he can cut down slightly on the amounts of these foods and add others more to his liking if he wishes, but, on the other hand, if he expects to do much camping out he must increase the quantity of such foods as can be used on the trail.

Judging from my own experience it is easier to choose good camp foods than to know which to use from the list for a meal and how to prepare them. On stormy days, or when for any other reason the camper is spending sufficient time at the main cabin, he can cook such foods as beans, split peas, rice, game, salt pork and dried fruits, also can make good use of the maple syrup and other luxuries. For short order meals, as, for instance, when returning to camp long past meal time and in a half famished condition, oatmeal porridge, bannock (baking powder bread), bacon and tea or coffee will generally satisfy. Here, for instance, is a good menu for a day when the hunter or trapper wants to make a journey away from the main camp, returning late in the afternoon. He rises early in the morning and prepares breakfast of coffee, pancakes, maple syrup and bacon, or, perhaps, has fried venison, moose or caribou steak. Immediately after breakfast he places over the fire a kettle of beans with a piece of salt pork and he boils this until he is ready to leave camp, which may be an hour later. While the beans are cooking and he is waiting for daylight he prepares the outfit which he will take with him for the day. His lunch will be creackers, or if not too cold a piece of bannock, a few slices of bacon, a small piece of cheese and tea. The bushman always carries a small tea pail with him, if only a tin can fitted with a wire bail. He returns about sunset and as soon as he has made a fire he places over it the partly cooked pork and beans. By the time they have finished cooking he has baked a bannock, stewed some fruit or prunes, or made rice pudding. Thus he goes on day after day, varying his menu as far as possible, as well as his methods of preparing the foods.

In the lists which I have given I have purposely refrained from naming the many prepared and condensed camp foods, because my experience with most of them has been limited and many of them I have never even tasted. I refer to such articles as dessicated vegetables, dried eggs, milk powder, erbswurst, pemmican, saccarine, tea tablets, soup tablets, etc.

Before closing I would like to say a few words in regard to game and fish as food. While I do not advise making much allowance for them when purchasing supplies the man who goes into the wilds to camp should avail himself of any opportunity which offers to secure game and fish for his use, but he should, of course, never kill more than is needed, and unless driven to it by hunger should not kill protected game out of season. If he kills more than he can use at the time and the weather is too warm to keep it without curing he should dry the meat and he will find it an excellent article for lunches and when camping out. But what I wanted to get at is this, that many animals which are seldom considered as fit for food and are generally thrown away or used for bait are really fine food and by using them there will be less need of violating the game laws. Among the animals which are trapped and may be used for food are bears (when killed in fall or winter), muskrats, raccoons, opossums and beavers. Woodchucks are not bad eating if properly cooked, but they can only be secured in summer. The porcupine is another animal which may be eaten, although I cannot say that the meat is palatable. Many people in Canada eat the flesh of lynx, but I draw the line on carnivorous animals. I have tried it, in fact, I have eaten all the animals named above.

My parting advice is to practice economy. The food which has been transported over so many miles of rough trail by the hardest kind of toil should never be wasted. The saving habit is a good one to grow into and it can be practiced as well in the woods as in our own homes.

FIRES FOR VARIOUS USES

Most fires to-day are started by means of matches, so, as a starting place we will first consider the match. Insignificant little stick—500 for five cents—yet that tiny match can start a fire that would destroy a city or lay a hundred miles of forest in ruin! Many a life has been saved by a match, and many millions, yes billions of dollars worth of property has been destroyed by the same insignificant little stick. It is on one hand one of the greatest providers of comfort that science has produced, and on the other the most powerful destroyer known to man. There are various kinds of matches, each having properties peculiar to itself, but we will compare only the most common kinds and judge them from the woodsman's standpoint.

I believe the first matches to come into use were made of a sulphurous compound and such matches are still used in large quantities in Canada. They are generally considered superior to ordinary parlor matches for woodsman's use, but I cannot see that they possess any advantages whatever. They are just as difficult to light as parlor matches, if not more so, just as easily blown out, and just as susceptible to dampness. They are noiseless, which is in their favor, but they throw off disagreeable fumes when lighted. They are reliable matches for the woodsman, although I would take parlor matches in preference.

We have also the little, so-called "safety" matches now so much used by smokers. They are convenient for carrying and get their name from their refusal to light when struck on any surface other than the side of the box in which they are packed. But this very quality makes them unfit to light a fire in a wind if one must hold in his hand the match-box as well as the burning match, for he cannot "cup" his hands perfectly. This is worth remembering, for out of doors, there is nearly always enough wind to make trouble when building a fire. Another fault of the safety match is its small size; it is apt to be entirely consumed before the fire can be started. The parlor match then is the match for the woodsman, and he should have a bountiful supply when he turns his back on civilization.

The stock of matches should be kept in a waterproof case of some kind. A screw top jar is very good if one has it in camp, but glassware is not practical for camping trips and something less fragile but equally waterproof should be found. I have a kodak tank developing outfit, the metal tank of which is excellent for holding matches. The cover locks on by a partial turn and is watertight, while the tank holds enough matches for a whole winter's use.

Of course the woodsman will carry with him on his sojourns from camp only a small quantity of matches and at least a few of them should either be so treated as to render them impervious to water, or be carried in a watertight box. It sometimes happens that the traveler in the woods gets caught in a drenching rain, or he may fall into the water, and unless some provision has been made for keeping the matches dry there will be no more smokes or tea until he gets back to camp. Sometimes more serious consequences may follow such negligence; for instance, the traveler may break through the ice and without a fire may freeze to death. Almost every outdoor man can recall instances where dry matches would at least have added materially to his comfort.

There are various ways of waterproofing matches. They may be dipped in melted paraffine, which will keep them perfectly dry, and when the protecting wax is removed they will be in first class condition. Varnishes of one kind or another will serve the same purpose.

But a waterproof box is more reliable and convenient.

A FIRE FOR RAINY DAYS.

There is one match-box on the market that is very efficient. It is somewhat difficult to open, especially when one's hands are cold, but for all of that it is the best thing I know of, and as its contents are to be used only in emergency cases the woodsman may be content with the box as it it. I have seen match-boxes made from brass shotgun shells which were practically waterproof if kept tightly closed, but sometimes it is difficult to remove the cover. A small glass bottle is also good for carrying matches and is frequently used for this purpose.

It is an easy matter to light a match; but to start a fire is something different, and to build a fire when the wind is blowing is often difficult. Even the simple lighting of a pipe in the wind is very uncertain with many smokers. I have seen men out in an exposed place strike match after match in a vain endeavor to light a pipe. Yet rightly done the trick is easy. It is all right to get behind a tree if one is near; but it is not at all necessary. In all cases the man should turn his face towards the wind and as soon as he strikes the match, form a cup of his hands and thus shelter the burning match. Then it is easy to thrust the bowl of the pipe into his hands to the burning match. A fire can be started in the same way, but it is a little more difficult and less certain. The kindling must be properly arranged with the part to be lighted projecting towards the breeze, and sufficiently separated from other objects, so that the fire builder may enclose this part in the shelter of his hands, along with the match, and thus protect the flame until the kindling is fairly lighted. Often a sheet of bark dropped against the tiny flame will protect it until it gathers strength. A dry surface on which to strike a match is essential and the woodsman must use his knowledge of suitable surfaces to help him out of his trouble. A pocket match-box usually has one side roughened for this purpose. A very practical idea is to sew a small strip of emery cloth on the inside of the coat, the upper half being loose so that it folds down over the other half and thus keeps the rough surface from contact with the clothing. The back of a pocket-knife, the butt plate of a gun, or a key may also be made to answer. Of natural surfaces the side of a stone or the dry trunk of a tree may serve. But the most common scheme is to utilize the trouser leg for striking matches and as long as the clothing is dry it is certainly the most convenient surface for this purpose.

When a match gets wet, if the head is not so much softened that it rubs off the stick, there is hope. Rubbing the match through the hair will dry it in an amazingly short time.

There is no right or wrong way to make a fire unless it is to be used for some special purpose, in which case we must know how the fire is to be used and build it accordingly. As a rule a cooking fire is built differently from one that is designed merely to give warmth. But we must always take into consideration the strength of the wind, whether the fire is for boiling, baking or frying food, and whether a quick or slow heat is wanted, for each and all call for a different kind of fire. The variety of wood and its condition must also be considered.

For most kinds of cooking only a small fire is required, in fact we get better results from a small flame. But it is essential that we have some arrangement whereby the cooking utensils will be held steadily and securely. The most common practice is to place the kettle or frying pan on top of the fuel, shifting the wood about until the utensils set level. It is about the most unsatisfactory method, outside of holding them by hand. and many a meal has been upset into the fire simply because the cook would not take the trouble to provide a suitable place to prepare the meal. The simplest way of suspending a kettle over the fire is by hanging it from the end of a stick which has been thrust into the ground at an angle of about 20 degrees. In the woods of the north this method is used generally for boiiing. When the bushman stops for tea, which is always the most essential and important part of his repast, he builds a fire, then cuts a stick an inch or a little more in thickness and about four feet long, and thrusts it into the ground in such a way that when the tea-pail is suspended from the end it hangs at just the right height above the fire. Only a small fire is required, but it should give a clear, steady flame, for the water should be brought to a boil quickly

For frying, baking, etc., I find an arrangement of two small green logs, flattened on top and bottom, and placed side by side about a half foot apart, the most satisfactory thing for holding the utensils securely. Between these logs a small fire is made, and there is no danger of the food spilling into the fire, or the handles of the utensils becoming so hot that they have to be moved with sticks. For a single utensil, like a frying pan, I find two straight-sided stones placed the right distance apart, fully as good as the logs, and only a few embers from the camp fire will be needed for the cooking.

Almost everybody who camps for the night builds a camp-fire, in fact, without it a camp would seem far from complete, even though the night is a warm one. Cooking, however, should be done over a smaller fire placed nearby.

There are a lot of little helpful wrinkles regularly used by woodsmen that can hardly be imparted to the green-hand because of their number, their insignificance, and the fact that each must be adapted to the prevailing condition, but they immediately brand the user as an old hand at the game. They are simply the result of experience and are used almost unconsciously. I refer to such things as the manner of placing wood on the fire, handling embers, moving cooking utensils, etc. It is the knowledge of how to do such little things as this that makes the work of the expert look so easy and run along so smoothly, while Mr. Amateur is having all kinds of trouble. There is no way to acquire this knowledge except by long experience, or by working in company with one who has "been there."

I know a way of building a very good combination heating and cooking fire, which may be used during rainy weather more satisfactorily than any other kind with which I am acquainted. Two small green logs about five feet long, are placed side by side about 20 inches apart. Two shorter logs are then placed across the ends and another five-foot log laid lengthwise on top. The fire is built between the two bottom logs and directly under the one which has been placed on top. Then pieces of green wood are stood up against one side so that they rest against the top and one of the bottom logs. This forms a roof over the fire and the cooking is done over the open front, between the logs. The roof burns away slowly on the under side and as the sticks burn off they are added to the fire beneath and others placed on top to keep the roof built up. This is a good style of fire to reflect heat into the camp and is excellent for use with a metal baker.

The regulation method of building a fire for heating an open-camp is to place it against a large green log, or against a ledge of rock, a wall of stones built up artificially, or a pile of short green logs resting against two stakes which have been driven at a slight incline. The fire burns best when there are two short pieces of wood placed crosswise on the ground on which the fuel may rest and leave an opening for draft beneath. Green wood is best for holding fire; but it must be mixed with good dry wood, or it will not burn well. The selection of wood for the camp-fire is important. Standing dead trees are always drier than those which have fallen, unless the fallen trees are held up sufficiently above the ground to keep them well dried. Wood cut on low, damp ground is not as good as that found on higher places and usually pops and throw sparks into the blankets, which make it objectionable.

Almost all kinds of dry, hard wood burn readily and throw off plenty of heat. They also burn to embers and hard wood therefore should be selected when a bed of live coals is needed. Of the soft wood dry pine and cedar burn freely, but are consumed quickly, leave no embers and make a lot of smoke. They are excellent wood for kindling and for use in connection with green, hard wood. Green pine, cedar, fir and tamarack burn slowly and require much dry wood to help keep them burning. White birch is excellent for camp-fires; dry or green and dry tamarack is one of the best of camp-fire woods.

There are various woods that answer well for kindling and the camper must always find something that will be good for this purpose. Dry white-pine and cedar shavings and splints light readily from the match, but dead "fat" pine is much better. Pine knots, remaining after the log has rotted away, when split are heavy and yellow with dried pitch and if split into

Regular cooking fire

—for making tea

for a bed
of coals

FIRES FOR COOKING.

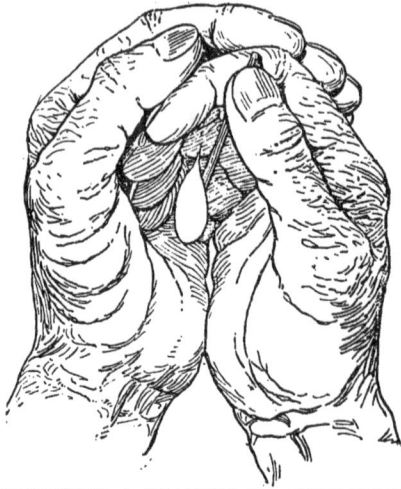

LIGHTING A MATCH IN THE WIND.

splinters will burn like oil. An old pine log is often in the same condition, and if the camper can find any wood of this kind he should take some to camp so that he will not need to hunt about for a suitable wood for starting a fire. In the north where there is little pine timber such kindling is scarce; but nature has provided an excellent substitute in white-birch bark. The loose bark hanging to the tree trunks contains an oil which causes it to light readily from the match and burn with a bright flame and a hissing noise. When traveling in the northern bush during cold weather I frequently carried a bunch of birch bark in the top of my pack, so that if I wanted to build a fire quickly I would not have to hunt for kindling.

There is one more woodcraft trick that I think everybody who goes into the woods should know. While the woodsman invariably carries an axe with which to cut firewood, there may come a time when he has no axe and is obliged to camp out over night. Then getting together sufficient wood to keep fire over night is a real problem. Sometimes he can find a place where one tree has fallen across another, or if not, perhaps he can throw one over the other, and at the place where they cross he should build his fire. Then when the logs burn through he can nove them and either keep shoving the ends into the fire as hey burn away, or perhaps cross the pieces again and burn them nto shorter and lighter pieces which can be handled readily.

In building any kind of a fire the camper should remember hat flame naturally moves upward, so that the wood should be ighted from beneath. It is hard to get a fire started in any other way. He should also remember that the wind drives the fire forward and should light the wood under the windward side. The finest kindling should be placed first, then finely split dry wood on top, coarser wood on top of this, etc. The heavy wood should never rest too much on the kindling or the latter will be crushed down into such a dense mass that it will not burn and the wood must never be placed so that the sticks fit closely together; a criss-cross style is much better. These are all simple little rules and easy to remember, but it is necessary to know them that camp-fire troubles may be avoided.

FIRE

The most common way of building a fire among savages who have not adopted the ways of civilization is by means of a bow, spindle and block.

This way of making fire has been exploited by writers on woodcraft subjects; but the reader should not be deceived into the belief that if he becomes lost in the woods and night coming on finds him without matches, he can build a fire by this means. While any boy scout can demonstrate the method and can produce fire in a very few minutes, he can do so only by having prepared the necessary materials long in advance. The wood must be as dry as wood can be made, and such wood is never found in the forest. To get wood into the proper condition for fire making by the friction method requires the selection first of the proper kind of wood, and then a thorough drying indoors for weeks or even months. Only certain kinds of woods are really good for the purpose and among these kinds cedar, balsam and cottonwood seem to be the best. Spindle and block must be of the same kind of wood and equally dry.

The materials needed for making a fire are the bow, spindle, block, tinder, and a shell, a stone with a small cavity, or other similar object which can be used as a bearing or cap on top of the spindle. A mussel shell is the best natural object for the

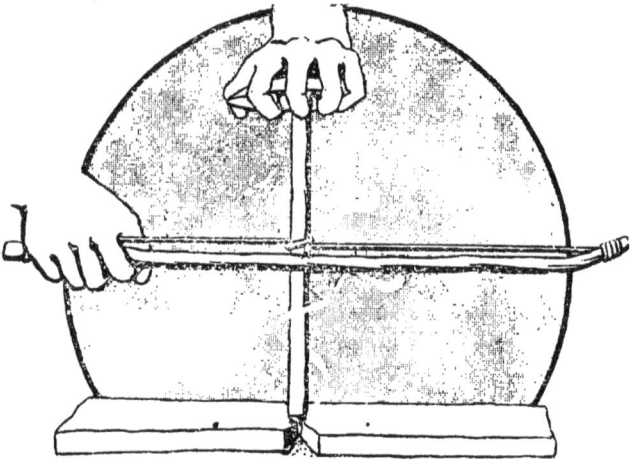

USING THE BOW DRILL IN MAKING FIRE.

purpose, as it is light and has a hollow side which is smooth and makes an excellent bearing for the spindle end.

The bow, about two feet long, may be made of hickory or any springy wood, strung with a stout, hard laid twine. The spindle, of any of the favorite woods, should be about sixteen inches long by three-fourths or one inch in thickness. The top should be rounded and the lower end shaped to a blunt, smooth point. It must be very dry. The block should be an inch or a little more in thickness and of any width and length found convenient, but it should be large enough to be easily held down firmly with the knees when in the kneeling position assumed when working the drill. It should be of the same kind of wood as the spindle. The tinder may be any inflammable material which can easily be fired from the burning dust, such as the shredded inner bark of a cedar tree, very dry and fine, mixed with shreds of white cotton cloth.

To use the outfit the operator cuts a V-shaped notch about three-quarters of an inch deep in the edge of the block. On the flat side of the block at the apex of the notch he then makes a small hole with the point of a knife as a starting place for the spindle. Around this notch he places a small quantity of the inder. Then, giving the string of the bow a turn around the spindle he kneels on the block, places the point of the spindle n the mark at the point of the notch, places the shell over the)ther end, and throwing his weight upon the spindle he works :he bow back and forth quickly and steadily. The spindle, revolving rapidly, bores its way down into the block, the dust which is worn from the block and spindle filtering down through the notch among the dry tinder. An increasing heat develops from the friction of the dry wood, and soon an odor of scorching wood will be noticed; then a thin wisp of smoke arises from the dust in the notch and this grows stronger, after awhile the smoldering fire itself is visible in the dust which has accumulated in the notch and about the base of the spindle. At this stage the operator stops the drill and blows the fire into flame. All that is necessary then is to place fine, dry twigs over the tinder and then coarser wood, and this wonderful feat of building a fire without matches is accomplished.

Matches are a comparatively recent invention. When this country was first settled they were unknown and fires generally were made by means of flint and steel. By striking glancing blows with a steel object along the edge of a piece of flint, showers of sparks were thrown into a little pile of tinder to be blown into a flame by the fire-kindler. It is said that for an expert the trick was not at all difficult, and that fire could be produced very quickly; but it is obvious that very dry materials were necessary.

To the unfortunate who is cast away on a desert island, like the hero of fiction, this latter method of fire making is the most promising, for he usually has some steel object, even if only a pocket knife and a piece of his coat lining picked into shreds may answer as tinder. The difficulty will be in finding the flint; but that is easy in the story.

But the easiest of all ways to make a fire without matches is by means of a magnifying glass or other lens. A reading glass, if the sun is bright, will produce a fire almost as quickly as it can be made with a match, providing, of course, that it is used the right way. In the absence of a reading glass, a watch or compass crystal, an eye glass, the lens from a field glass or camera, or even a bottle, may be used for concentrating the sun's rays onto a pile of tinder and thus producing a fire. If you are sceptical as to the heat caused by a concentrated light ray, just hold a reading glass a few inches above your hand and

USING THE FLINT AND STEEL TO START A FIRE.

turn the glass towards the sun so that a tiny point of intense light is thrown onto your hand and you will be surprised to see how quickly it will burn a blister. A pipe may be lighted that way very easily, something that is worth knowing if one happens to get caught in the woods without matches and with a magnifying glass in his pocket.

But he may not have a glass of any description and then—well here is another way: A man traveling in the woods nearly always carries a gun of some kind. Let him remove the bullet from a cartridge and substitute a small bunch of dry tinder; shredded dry cotton cloth is as good as anything, and loading this cartridge into the gun, fire it into another small pile of tinder and blow the smoldering pile into a flame.

The safest and most convenient way of all is, of course, to carry matches, and to have a portion of them in a waterproof box. Matches are cheap and a waterproof box will not bankrupt a woodsman. I always, when in the woods, carry matches in a waterproof match box, and I never use them except in emergency, carrying my regular supply loose in a small pocket.

There was one time that I well remember when that box of dry matches was to me about the most valuable thing in the

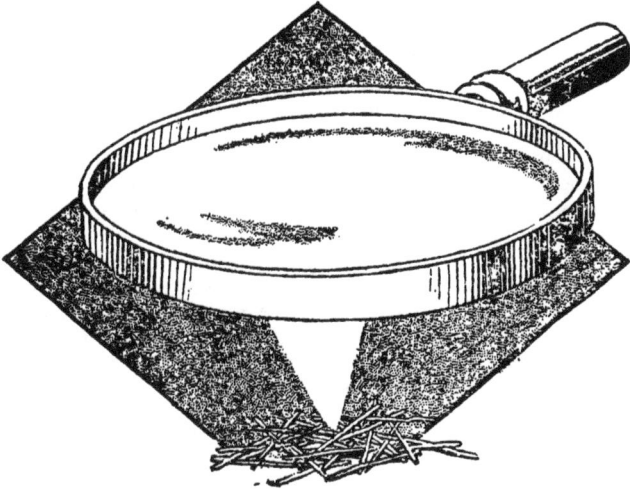

STARTING A FIRE WITH A MAGNIFYING GLASS.

world. That was the time when I broke through the ice of a lake in the northern wilderness, far from camp, and my clothes froze stiff before I had gone a hundred paces. The dry matches enabled me to make a fire quickly and dry my frozen clothes. What could I have done without the waterproof match box?

Fire is as useful to the modern woodsman as it was to the prehistoric man and in the far north it stands between him and death when King Boreas reigns. But it can also do a world of mischief. Is it not strange that the great forces which are so terribly destructive when let loose in all their strength are the most beneficial and useful to mankind? We could not exist more than a few days without water, yet floods destroy each year millions of dollars worth of property and thousands of lives. Electricity is, perhaps, the most useful power in the world and we have grown so used to it that to give up its comfort, which we derive in the form of light, power and heat, would be an awful hardship, and yet electricity is the most dangerous and deadly element known.

Fire also is so needful that we could no longer exist without it. It alone can make our homes comfortable when the winter winds howl without. Its heat is necessary for the preparation of the greater portion of our food. Yet fire is a dangerous and destructive element, and must be closely watched at all times to prevent it from breaking out of bounds. From the harmless comforter of the home it becomes the relentless destroyer.

The loss by fire would be reduced greatly if all persons would observe a few simple rules and in the hope that some of the readers may become just a little more careful in this respect I will give these rules here:

(1) Use only "safety" matches. They will ignite only by friction on the preparation found on the side of the box in which they are purchased. If one of these matches falls on the floor it is harmless since it cannot light accidentally and thus cause a fire. If they fall into the hands of children they are also harmless as far as starting a fire is concerned.

(2) Do not throw a lighted match onto the floor, or among rubbish. Burned matches should always be placed somewhere where they cannot possibly ignite anything in case a little fire still smolders in the burned wood.

(3) Don't drop cigarettes or cigar ends into places where they can do harm, and if there appears to be the least possible danger they should be carefully extinguished. A pipe dumped into a waste basket has many times started costly fires.

(4) Be sure that there is no woodwork so near the stove that it grows scorching hot when the stove is overheated. Likewise make sure that no rubbish is thrown near the stove or fireplace and that there is no danger of fire dropping out onto the floor.

(5) Never leave the house with a fire burning in the stove, or fireplace.

(6) Kerosene and similar substances should never be used for kindling fires; their use is exceedingly dangerous. Gasoline especially is very dangerous, not alone through the fact that it is very inflammable but even more so from the fact that the fumes of gasoline explode with great violence. It should never be used in a house where there is a fire or a lighted lamp, and a fire should never be lighted in a room where it has been used until the fumes are completely cleared from the room.

Burning oil can be extinguished by smothering with woolen blankets, or by throwing sand on it. Water merely spreads the fire.

While fires in settled communities do the most damage, a dry season may see many destructive forest fires. Such conflagrations destroy the forests and kill game and song birds, besides being a menace to settlers. This country suffers great losses through forest fires, many of which could be prevented by an observance of the rules already given, especially those relating to smoking. Campers are also responsible for many fires of this kind by failing to extinguish camp fires, or by building them in places where rubbish abounds. A camp fire should never be made except on a spot of clean ground and if necessary a spot should be cleared before building the fire, digging away the vegetable matter on the surface, if need be. Likewise the camper should be certain that there is no danger from the fire spreading before he leaves it.

Ordinarily he can feel sure of this only when he has completely extinguished the fire by pouring water upon it.

BLANKETS

One of the first things to learn is that blankets, no matter how good, are not "warm," they don't generate heat. Wrap a jar of water in the warmest, thickest, softest woolen blanket you can find and place it out of doors over night in a zero temperature and see what you have in the morning. No, there is no warmth coming from the blankets, but the warmth comes from the human body and the purpose of the blanket is to retain this warmth, to prevent its escape. It must therefore be a non-conductor of heat. And remember that there is no such thing as cold, for what we call cold is merely an absence of heat, and we call it cold for convenience.

Suppose you are sleeping, or attempting to sleep out of doors on a night so cold that the trees pop like pistols. You are wrapped in a pair of woolen blankets and it is only this wrapping that is between you and the frosty, chilling air. But inside of those blankets your body is giving out heat waves, the air on the inside becomes warm, and you are comfortable. Suppose again that the blankets are not the right kind, they will not retain heat, and as a consequence you become cold. You sit up, replenish the fire and swear to yourself, but you don't know why you can't keep warm. You say the cold gets through your blankets and you firmly believe this. As a matter of fact it is the heat that gets through, not the cold.

Outside of fur the best heat-retaining material used for blankets is pure wool. A little cotton may do no noticeable harm, if properly used in conjunction with the wool, but it certainly does no good, and it really decreases the warmth of the blanket in direct proportion to the quantity used, therefore I say the best blankets are made of pure wool. And there is a difference in wool, too. Scotch wool is generally admitted to be the finest produced.

It has always been my belief that wool loosely woven, so that it forms a soft, thick cloth, is a better heat retainer than the same quantity of wool tightly woven, so that it makes a thinner, tighter and harder material. Anyway, I think the surface should be as woolly as it is possible to make it.

Now it is not difficult to get together a quantity of blankets that will keep a man warm on the coldest night, but the trouble will come when he wants to transport them. I have slept out on nights when it would have required a half-dozen or more of the heaviest woolen blankets made to keep me near-comfortable, but a bed of this kind would have made a pack that would discourage a bush Indian. No, you can't carry with you enough woolen blankets to keep you comfortably warm when traveling the northern trails in midwinter. Now think it over and it will become obvious that either a man cannot be comfortable in the woods during zero weather unless he has a way of transporting his camp duffle other than by back-packing, or he must find a lighter, warmer blanket than can be made of wool. The latter is the solution.

Woolen blankets are good, in fact the best thing made, for camping in spring, summer and fall. As long as the spirits do not go lower than 10 or 20 degrees above zero and a fire may be kept burning all night a pair of Hudson Bay blankets are hard to beat. But when the temperature falls lower the shivering spells preceding each "fire-fixing" become too frequent and the cat-naps too short.

The blankets we buy for use on the bed are double, but for camp use single blankets are preferable. They should be of generous size, for a white man cannot sleep comfortably if he must draw his knees up against his chin. What is more, the blankets should cover his head as well as his feet, so they should be a foot and a half longer than the user's height. They should also be wide—six feet will do, but nothing less. With such blankets a man can lie on one-half and pull the other half over him, and by suddenly elevating his pedal extremities he can drop the lower edge of the blankets under them, while the upper part can be drawn tightly around his head and shoulders. Thus he can sleep in real comfort while the fire burns.

Never use a cotton blanket in the woods. Blankets made of cotton are cold to the touch, and do not retain the heat of the body as well as those made of wool. In addition to this they have the bad fault of not being as nearly impervious to sparks as woolen blankets. Now a man of the trail does not sleep with his feet towards the fire like the pioneer scout of border fiction, but he lies by the side of the fire, where he will get the benefit of its heat, and sometimes he rolls closer than he should for safety.

This I learned from actual experience about the first time I ever tried camping out. I believed firmly that I couldn't afford to buy woolen blankets, so I used a pair made of cotton. I was sleeping by the side of a fire and as it was quite cold I snuggled close. I awoke to find a decidedly warm feeling about my knee, and on hasty examination found a large section of one trouser leg burned away and a hole in the blanket over a foot in diameter. I then decided that I could afford woolen blankets and have stood by that decision ever since.

One of the best blankets for camping purposes that I ever owned was a square horse blanket, from which I removed the trimmings. Its thick all-wool body and generous size made it ideal for camp use. The Hudson's Bay blankets are excellent, being heavy and of large size. Then there are many camp blankets of less note, most of which are good. Really good, heavy, all-wool blankets of a size 72x84 inches will cost from $5.00 to $10.00 each for single blankets, and twice that much for the double kind, if you can get them. These single blankets should weigh from four and a half to five pounds each. Color is immaterial—if you fancy the bright scarlet kind buy it, for it will give as good service as a gray one. But a white blanket is almost sure to contain all good wool, for it is harder to conceal shoddy stuff that is not dyed. White is not a good color for camping purposes, but it is not a difficult task to dye a white blanket.

A woolen blanket is neither heavy, bulky, nor stiff. It is easily folded to fit the pack, and when properly arranged it forms a pad which protects the back of the packer from the corners of the cooking utensils and the ever-gouging steel traps and other hardware. If the packer has no pack cloth he can use the blanket for this purpose, although it is none too good for the blanket. If it gets wet it is easily dried without danger of burning, and if it does not get thoroughly dry it is warmer still than a cotton blanket.

But when zero weather is to be contended with woolen blankets must take a back seat for the Indian's kind, woven from strips of rabbit fur. Nothing that I have ever found will equal or even approach in warmth a rabbit skin blanket. One such blanket, weighing eight or ten pounds, is all that a man requires for sleeping out of doors in a temperature of 40 below zero. Yes, I know that it sounds far-fetched; but a trial will convince the most skeptical. Many a morning I have found my nose almost frozen when I awoke, but otherwise I was perfectly comfortable; the reason being that my nose was the only part of my anatomy not enveloped in the rabbit skin blanket. I couldn't believe that it was so cold until I emerged from the folds of the covering to kindle a fire. With one of these fur blankets I have slept comfortably off and on during an entire winter north of Lake Superior, in a cabin which had the cracks chinked on two sides only, the other two sides having openings between the logs through which I could put my hand, and I never had a fire at night.

These blankets are made by all northern Indian tribes. They are woven from the skins of the snowshoe rabbit, or varying hare, cut into strips for the purpose. The animals producing these skins are found in almost incredible numbers in most of the wilder parts of Canada, as well as in parts of the northern States. The blankets can be made only in winter, when the fur is white and in good condition. The rabbits are taken in snares, case skinned, and the skins are cut into strips while green. This work is done by the squaws. The method is to trim the open end of the skin, then starting at this end with a sharp knife the entire skin is cut into a single strip about an inch wide by holding it on the knee and cutting around and around. Each skin will make a strip 10 or 12 feet long. As soon as it is cut the skin rolls up like a cord, fur on all sides. These strips of green fur are wound into a ball and placed out of doors, where they will freeze and remain frozen, each day's accumulation being added to the ball until a sufficient number have been secured to make a blanket. I cannot say how many skins are required, but believe about 50 or 60, perhaps more. Of course the number needed would depend partly on the size of blanket desired.

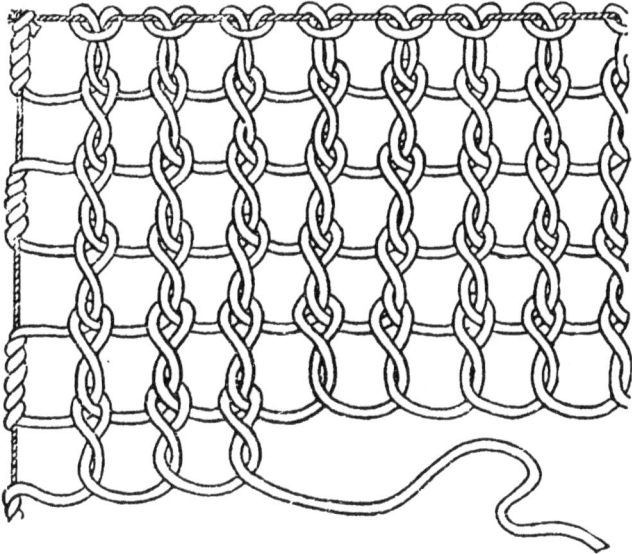

THIS SKETCH SHOWS HOW THE RABBIT SKIN
BLANKET IS MADE.

Now when Mrs. Indian has secured enough skins to form the
desired blanket she makes a square frame of poles, about the
size the finished blanket is to be, and fastens around the inside
a piece of heavy twine. Then sewing the end of a fur strip to
the cord at one of the upper corners she weaves this strip across
the end of the frame by looping it around the cord in a succes-
sion of simple loops, using her finger as a gauge to make the
mesh a uniform size. When a gauge reaches the end of the
strip she sews on another and weaves it as before. When she
has made such a row of little loops all across the top of the
frame she passes the fur strip around the side cord a few times
and then starts another row backward, looping the strip into the
row of loops already formed. Thus she weaves the strips of
fur back and forth across the frame until the robe is finished.
These simple loops will not slip after the fur has become dry.
The entire blanket must be perfectly dry before it is removed

from the frame, and it must never be allowed to become wet. The skins are not tanned, simply dried.

These blankets are usually wider at one end than at the other, so that there will be sufficient width to wrap around the shoulders of the user and yet no more material, bulk and weight than necessary. I find it most satisfactory to double the blanket lengthwise and loop a cord through the edges across the foot and a third of the way up the side, thus fastening the edges firmly together and making it somewhat like a sleeping bag. So made I do not get my feet uncovered at night, and yet it is easy to get into and out of it. These blankets, or robes as they are sometimes called, are so loosely woven that a man can put his fingers through anywhere, yet for their weight they are the warmest bedding I know of.

I believe an ordinary rabbit blanket will weigh about eight pounds. It appears bulky, for with fur on both sides it is quite thick, but it can be tied up into a fairly small package. I used to roll mine into a package measuring about 10 inches in diameter by 20 inches in length, and this could be placed in the bottom of a common packsack. There it formed a soft pad for the back and the heavy articles were thrown higher up in the pack, where the weight should be, if weight is ever really needed in a pack.

I fancy I hear somebody asking how this species of bedding is to be kept dry in rainy weather. If it is warm enough for rain a rabbit robe is not needed—that is the time to use the woolen blanket. It never rains during cold weather. In the north, where these fur blankets are needed and used, the weather turns cold in November, remaining so until March or April, and during this time it is considered remarkable if it ever becomes warm enough to rain. I have never had one of these blankets wet, except that nearly every morning the fur on the outside will be more or less wet, presumably from the moisture which it throws out to the surface. This is only on the outside fur and will soon dry off if the blanket is hung where the warmth from the fire can reach it.

The only fault I find with these fur blankets is that they are continually shedding the hair, and rabbit hair is apt to appear in the biscuits, and is certain to be sprinkled plentifully over the clothing. This is not so objectionable to outdoor men, but it prohibits the use of the article in the house.

Any trapper living in the northern forest should be able to make a rabbit skin blanket for his own use. A few days setting and tending snares will provide the necessary number of rabbits, and the weaving of the blanket may be done on a cold day or in the evenings. I have never made one, for I have been able to buy them from the Indians at prices ranging from $6.00 to $10.00 each, and that is cheaper than I could make one myself.

The camp bed that is generally unloaded on the unsuspecting tenderfoot is some form of sleeping bag. There may be good sleeping bags and it is possible that I am unduly prejudiced against this form of camp bed, for I have given only two styles a real tryout, but I can say emphatically that the kinds I used were no good. My first sleeping bag was made of heavy canvas, inside of which was a separate bag made of a blanket. It was very unsatisfactory, for in addition to being exceedingly stiff and inconvenient for handling, getting into and out of it, it was also a very poor protection against the cold.

The next investment along this line was one of the sheep-skin-lined bags advertised so much about 10 or 15 years ago. It was made of heavy duck with a lining of sheepskin with the wool on. Inside of this was a blanket bag and this was also fitted with a removable drill sack, which could be washed. If weight and thickness were sure indications of warmth this should have been all right for the polar regions, for the complete outfit must have weighed 25 pounds. I found it very little warmer than the bag with the blanket lining, and I was not long in getting rid of it.

This is the extent of my experience with sleeping bags, but it is sufficient to turn me against the entire family. As I said before there may be good ones, but I am from Missouri. The plain, heavy, all-wool blanket for me as long as the weather is not bitterly cold, for when zero temperature comes I want a rabbit fur blanket if I am to do much camping out. These are good enough for me until I find something better, and I don't expect to find it. They have been with me under the most trying conditions and have proved their worth.

What is needed by the trapper, or by anybody who finds occasion to camp out, is something light with little bulk that will keep him as warm and comfortable as he can hope to be under the circumstances. This he finds in the articles recommended.

Other furs than that of the rabbit have been tried out for blankets, but I am told that they are not as good. Lynx and wolf fur are perhaps the best kinds, as they are long and dense, while the skin is relatively light. But they are all heavier than rabbit fur, less warm and much more costly.

A deer skin makes a nice spread for the top of the camp

bed to sleep on when the weather is cold, for it stops much of the cold air that comes up through the bed from beneath and helps retain the heat generated by the body of the occupant. The skin need not be tanned.

A man needs a night cap of some kind when sleeping out of doors. I have slept quite comfortably when wearing a wool toque, and I have also used the loose hood, which is worn by most northern bushmen to keep the snow from getting inside of the clothing. Some men can get along very well with an ordinary hat or cap.

In the bushman's outfit, as I see it, the blanket is second in importance only to the ax. How can good, pure wool be used more advantageously than in the form of a blanket, which will keep the owner comfortable eight or nine hours out of each 24? The worth of a blanket to the man of the woods can hardly be over-estimated. And when its days of usefulness as a blanket are ended it will still bring him much more comfort by being converted into mittens, hood, and extra protection for the feet when the Frost King reigns.

THE WOODSMAN'S AX AND ITS USE

On the ax more than on anything else depends the comfort and success of the northern forest traveler, whatever his calling. He may, to lighten his load, discard all of the articles in his outfit which are not absolutely essential, but never by any chance is the ax among those cast aside, because this tool is the most necessary and the most useful article used by the bushman. Not a day passes that the ax is not put to strenuous use, and on the trap line nearly every hour of the day finds the ax at work, smoothing the rough path of the traveler and providing for his comfort and welfare.

How could the wilderness trapper exist without the aid of this most useful tool? On it he must depend for his night's supply of firewood, and when the weather is cold this means not only comfort, but life itself, for the hardiest trapper could not long survive a temperature of forty below without a good warm fire beside which to spread his bed. With the ax he cuts poles for the frame work of his night's camp; he uses it to blaze the trail that he may follow it again when he goes the rounds to glean his harvest from the traps which he has set; he uses it when making the sets themselves; for cutting the drooping, snow-laden branches across his trail, and many minor uses which cannot now be mentioned. When making a hard trip he may leave his gun in camp, and may even travel and camp without blankets, shelter or cooking utensils, but the ax must go with him on every trip.

We are told that in early days the Indians paid fabulous prices for the most simple and common tools, and it has been said that as much as a hundred dollars in furs has been paid by an Indian hunter for an ax. It seems like wholesale robbery, but the bargain had two sides—two points of view. The Indian simply exchanged what was practically worthless to him for what was of priceless value, and from his point of view he drove as shrewd a bargain as did the trader. When we leave civilization behind us values change, and utilitarian worth counts more than intrinsic value, therefore, the ax becomes more valuable than a whole season's catch of furs.

If any class of people need perfect goods it is the class who must depend on these goods for their existence. The woodsman should have a perfect gun, perfect traps, perfect camp equipment, the best food he can buy, but above all a perfect ax. It should be of the finest material and of the best temper, tough but not hard. When put to a great strain steel will do one of two things—it will bend or it will break. If of good quality, with the proper proportion of carbon, it will stand an unusually severe test before it will do either, but when it does give it should bend rather than break. Of this kind of steel the trapper's ax should be made, and it should have a temper which will enhance these good qualities. If the ax is tempered a little too hard the edge will break when cutting into hard knots or frozen wood, or when the frost has not been drawn from the edge before using. When once the edge becomes dulled it is difficult to sharpen, for the trapper of the great woods has no grindstone, and must depend on file and whetstone to keep his cutting tools in perfect condition. A hard ax cannot be filed, so that puts the taboo on the ax with high temper.

I have emphasized the necessity for perfection in the trapper's ax, and that you may realize the seriousness of this, I will repeat what I said at the beginning of this article, that often the camper's life depends on the ax and its ability to stand the woodsman's test. The northern or western trapper frequently finds it necessary to make long trips in terribly cold weather, camping out night after night. Since the entire camp outfit and food supply must be carried on these journeys the outfit taken must of necessity be meager. Only a single blanket and a small, light canvas shelter can be taken and to sleep without a fire under such conditions is out of the question. A good hot fire must be kept going and such a fire will consume nearly half a cord of wood during the long northern night. This must be cut into lengths that can be handled and what would become of the camper if his ax were to break before the night's wood was cut; he far from the home camp, darkness at hand, and the temperature far below the zero mark. Freezing to death could be the only possible outcome, unless he could retrace his steps in the dark and travel all the long night. So you see it will pay you to test your ax well before you take it into the woods, and take only one that will stand the most severe trial, even if you break a dozen axes before you get one that is satisfactory.

What I have said of the material of the ax head applies with equal force to the ax handle. It should be of sound, strong, straight-grained, springy wood, for sometimes a broken ax handle is as disastrous as a broken blade. I have never found a better wood for ax handles than good second-growth hickory, but young white oak, the sapwood, is almost as good.

Even if the temper and material of the ax and handle leave nothing to be desired, if the ax is not of the right pattern, weight and length, it will be unsatisfactory. Perhaps the most useful pattern for the wilderness trapper is that having a long narrow blade, but this should not be carried to the extreme, as a narrow blade is more easily broken. The long blade is very useful when cutting holes into the sides of trees for setting marten traps or in making deadfalls, and for many similar uses about camp where the simplicity of the outfit necessitates making of the ax a general utility tool. If made extremely long and narrow, however, the consequent weakening and the fact that a narrow blade is not so satisfactory for hewing and for chopping in heavy wood more than offset the good qualities of the long blade. The eye of the ax should be large, so that the handle may be large in the eye of the ax and close by the head, and it should be enlarged slightly at both edges. This will make it possible to wedge the handle so that it will hold the head solidly, and it will leave the handle if fitted well, thickest where the greatest strain comes, close to the eye of the ax.

In the shaping of an ax blade there are some rules that must be remembered and adhered to if the maximum of efficiency is

POSITION OF AX WHEN CUTTING BRUSH

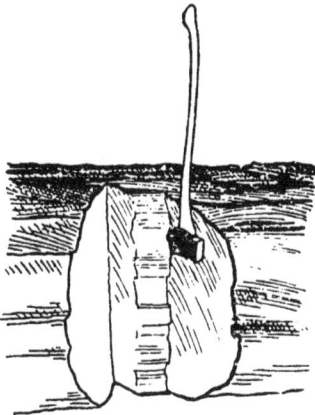

CUTTING THE FIRST NOTCH.

THE WOODMAN'S PERFECT AX.

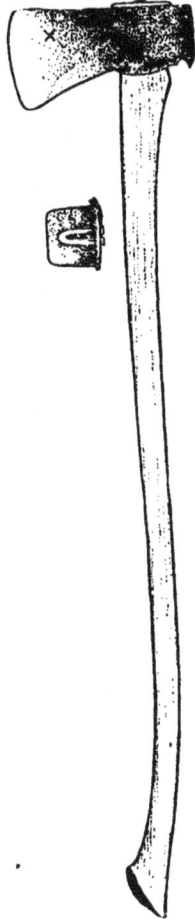

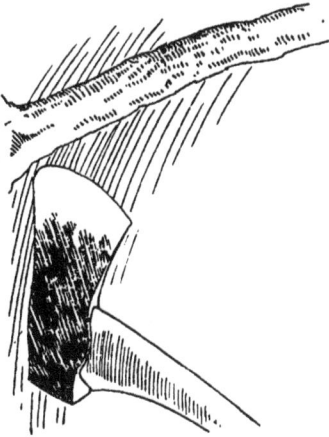

desired. These same rules must be known to the user of the tool, for in the grinding, a bad chopping ax may often be made better, while bad grinding makes it worse. One of these rules, and the most important, is to have the blade or bit thinnest on the "inside corner," which is the end of the blade nearest to the user. The hasty conclusion would be that if this corner were thinnest, the opposite side of the blade should be thickest. This is wrong. The thickest part of the blade should be two-thirds of the way across from the inside corner, the place marked X in the drawing of what I call "the woddsman's perfect ax." A blade so shaped will have the maximum chopping power, will sink easily into the tree, will burst the chip well, and will not bind in the wood.

I think it best that the ax head be made of wrought iron, split, and a welded-in steel bit. This gives the maximum strength. The butt of the ax might also be of steel, and would be more convenient for the trapper if it had a claw for drawing trap staples. If the eye of the ax is not tempered in the least the entire head may be made of steel and will be almost, if not fully, as strong, while the making is simplified.

You may wonder why a trapper need concern himself with the making of the ax if he can buy it ready made, but if there is a trapper's perfect ax made, I do not know of it. I know, however, that many readers of this article have in their locality a blacksmith who is fully capable of making such an ax to order.

For the northern forest and the western mountain district the ax that I would recommend would weigh only about two pounds, handle not included in the weight. Some of you may think this entirely too light, but the northern Indians use axes of only one and a half pounds, and find them heavy enough for practical purposes, while light to carry on the trail. To make a light ax effective, however, it must have a long handle. An ax like this should have a handle of from thirty to thirty-four inches over all, and with such a tool you will be surprised to see what heavy work can be done.

As said before, I do not know of a better wood for ax handles than hickory. It is very strong and springy and it always stays smooth; as cold to the touch as the ax head itself. It is difficult to get ax handle wood when we reach the upper part of the northern tier of states or Canada, for hickory is not found there. Hard maple is used extensively for ax handles in these places; but it does not compare well with hickory. About the only way to get a handle of the proper length for the woodsman's ax is to remove the handle from a large ax and work it over into the proper shape and thickness. The full size single bit axes usually have clubs of handles and there is plenty of wood on which to work.

Did you ever wonder why an ax handle is curved in an S shape? It is made to fit the hands of the user without strain on the arms or wrists, and this curved shape enables him to hold the ax more solidly when striking a blow than could be done with a straight handle. The handle should be quite thick and "hand-fitting" near the end where it is grasped by the left hand (or right, according to whether the user is right or left handed), but the other part should be shaped so the hand can slide easily back and forth while chopping.

The handle should be fastened into the ax with a wedge, which in turn is held in place by a screw. The wedge has a head so that when the screw is removed it is easily pried out, and then if it is necessary to remove the handle the ax can be driven into the top of a stump or into a log, and the handle easily detached. Such wedges may be bought from almost any hardware company.

This is my idea of what a woodsman's ax should be, and such a tool weighing two pounds, with a well-shaped handle thirty or thirty-two inches long from the end to the ax eye makes an efficient tool of light weight and a great article for use on the trail or trap line. I might say of it, as Davy Crockett said of his knife: "It will jump higher, dive deeper, shave more hogs and stand more bending without breaking than any other made."

As nearly all woodsmen are good axmen, it may seem superfluous to give advice regarding the care of an ax, the way to grind it, and how to use it, but this article is not intended for those who know, but for these who do not, and are desirous to learn. By a reckless, careless blow at a hemlock knot I have seen the entire bit broken off an ax, while other axes of no better temper but properly ground and well handled have gone through an entire season of "bark peeling" without a nick of any consequence. I have seen axes ruined in a half day's work cutting brush close to the ground, and have myself used an ax day after day at the same kind of work without making a nick which could not be whetted out in a few minutes with a small ax stone.

There is also a lot of danger in the careless use of an ax.

I have known of at least two men who have cut their heads by splitting wood under a clothes line. The same thing may happen when working under a tree with low, drooping branches. In the woods it will pay double to make it a rule on every occasion to be sure that there is not even the smallest twig in the way to catch the ax before you make a stroke with it. Trim all brush away from around a tree before you commence to cut it, and observe the same precautions when you cut it into lengths or when lopping the branches. When cutting the fallen tree into lengths, the common and most convenient way is to stand on the log and chop it half way through between the feet, then turn and cut the other side in the same way. Use double precaution when doing this, for I have known of an ax being deflected and a nasty cut being the result. It seems that the smallest branch or sprout can turn the ax toward the foot of the chopper.

When chopping down timber the tree can nearly always be thrown either of three ways—the way the tree inclines or to either side, but not the opposite way from its inclination. In addition to the incline of the tree, the influence of the wind and the weight of the branches must be considered, and when all of these forces are brought to bear the timber cutter must be well "onto his job" to know just how to cut the tree to make it fall in the desired direction. A good chopper, however, can throw the tree to any spot designated within the falling zone almost every time. The wind is a great factor and must be considered, especially when the breeze is strong or when the tree appears to stand perfectly straight. A tree on a slope that appears to be perpendicular will, in nearly every case, fall down hill if free to fall as it wills, providing there is no contrary wind. If the tree really stands perfectly upright and there is no wind, it will fall best toward the side that has the most branches, or to the side having the greatest weight. If allowance must be made, however, for both wind and gravity, it is then the judgment of the chopper is put to the test. If he can estimate accurately the power of each of these forces, he can drop his tree exactly where he wants to, but how?

It is very simple. In cutting a tree a notch is cut on the side toward which the tree is to fall. Remember that this notch should be cut into the center of the tree, and when finished, should be exactly at a right angle to the line on which the tree is to fall. A notch is then cut on the opposite side, just a little higher on the tree, and when this notch is cut in almost to the center the tree will fall. If the tree is notched to fall the way it inclines and there is nothing to prevent it going that way, the second notch should be cut exactly parallel to the first. If, however, the tree leans a little to one side, if there are more branches on that side, or if the wind blows in that direction, the second cut should not be parallel with the first, but should be farther from it on the side from which the wind comes, so that there will be more wood to break on that side. In no case should the notches entirely meet on the other side, for if they do, should the tree be cut entirely off on one side, it will settle farther over to that side. Just how near you dare cut it off on the one side and how much you must hold on the opposite side can be learned only from experience.

There are other little things that have a certain amount of influence. For instance, if there is nothing to interfere, the tree in falling will draw slightly toward the high side of the notch first cut. Then, too, if the notch is not perfectly cut, if it is more acute on one side than on the other, as the tree falls the top and bottom of the notch will meet on one side before they do on the other, and this is certain to swing the tree slightly toward the wide or obtuse side of the notch. A heavy weight of branches, too, on one side may cause the tree to roll slightly in falling.

For your own safety it is always best to get back a safe distance from the tree when it starts to fall, because if it falls over a rock, a log, or a little rise in the ground the butt of the tree will kick and may lift your head off, which would be decidedly unpleasant. If there are other trees in the way, look out for falling branches.

I have already told how to cut the tree in sections, but the branches must be trimmed off before it can be cut up entirely. In trimming, work from the butt toward the top, as the branches usually grow that way, cut easier, and are not in the way while chopping. Hold the ax rigidly when trimming, as the knots are likely to be hard and an ax that is not held firmly may break or bend. Make it a rule to do no more trimming than necessary on such woods as hemlock and fir, which have very hard knots. Frozen wood is also likely to break the ax.

When splitting wood strike straight and don't try to spring the split open by prying with the ax, for that is the easiest way I know to break an ax handle. Usually it is easier and better to merely start the split with the ax and finish opening it up with wooden wedges, using the ax only to drive the wedges and to cut the contrary fibres. Just how to split a block easiest can be learned only from experience. Sometimes it is best to go right at a knot or the toughest place, and sometimes you must attack the clearest place, depending on circumstances. Ordinarily a piece of wood splits easiest by starting the end of the block with the ax and following up with a pair of wedges, using the ax to cut the binding splints.

Learn to cut close to the ground without striking the stones. It requires care, that is all, but one careless stroke may mean a badly damaged ax and an hour or more of hard work to make it sharp again. Don't strike downward when cutting brush; grasp the shrub, if a small one, with the left hand, and cut it by a single stroke, as illustrated, using the ax with one hand only. If the shrub is a large one, handle the ax with both hands and cut close to the ground, making a strong, slashing blow.

Grinding an ax requires some care, but it is really quite easy and it is surprising how many axmen will not attempt to grind an ax. I have known many good choppers, working in log camps, who could not grind an ax, or at least thought they could not.

As the ax comes from the store it usually has a decided bevel on the edge, and the first grinding means considerable work, for this bevel must be ground entirely away. Start well back on the blade and grind it slightly rounding down to the edge, until the edge is clean and even, then grind the other side in the same way. Some axmen maintain that the ax cuts better, or to use the woodsman's expression, "draws" better if in finishing the grinding the ax is given a wabbling motion. Keep in mind what I said about the shape of the blade, and if it is not already the proper form, try to improve it each time you put it on the grindstone. After grinding, whet the edge thoroughly with a fine whetstone until the scratched effect caused by grinding has given place to a smooth surface and a clean keen edge. If you do not whet it after grinding, the edge will crumble away and the ax will cut "dead."

The first grinding will tell you whether the ax is hard or soft. You can tell by the sound of it and by its grip on the grindstone. If it is soft it cuts rapidly, grips the stone hard and gives a dull. dead sound. If hard, it gives a ringing sound and the stone glides smoothly under it, cutting slowly and wearing the steel bright.

The woodsman cannot take a grindstone into the woods and the best substitute is a file. I always choose a flat mill file about eight inches long. Always push the file from well back on the bit down to the edge, and never from the edge towards the eye of the ax, or you will be almost certain to cut your hands before you have finished. After the filing, whet the ax until you have a smooth, sharp edge.

It will be evident that an ax that must be kept sharp with a file and whetstone must not be too hard, for a file will not cut hard steel. The axes sold by the Hudson's Bay Company to the Indian trappers are very soft, so that they may be filed easily, and the Indian files only on the edge, so that the ax soon has a bevel almost equal to a chisel. The average Indian takes just about as much care of an ax as a woman does of a butcher knife.

As the minister says, "Just one word more," and that is in regard to carrying the ax on the trail. I have tried many ways, but do not find anything more satisfactory than having a leather pouch to slip over the head of the ax and tucking it head down in the pack. When drawing a toboggan it is slipped under the binding cords. If I am carrying my outfit and do not have a gun, I carry the ax in my hand, which is the most satisfactory way on such occasions. The Indian thrusts his ax through his sash, handle to the rear and blade down, but I never fancied that way of carrying an ax.

SNOWSHOES—HOW TO MAKE THEM

My first efforts at snowshoe making came about through trying to repair the broken filling of a pair of Indian made snowshoes. In removing the winding from the toe cord I accidentally discovered the place where the filling had been tied at the finish of the last round. This filling was badly worn and I reasoned that if I could remove it in the reverse order from that in which it had been strung I would know how to weave the intricate web of a snowshoe. I tried it out, successfully filling the old frames, and while it was far from perfect work I had at least learned the secret of snowshoe weaving.

Removing the stringing from a pair of snowshoes, carefully noting every turn, twist and loop, is the best way to learn how the filling is strung, but not every person who has ambitions along this line has a pair of snowshoes so much worn that he would care to risk removing the rawhide strands. Clearly written instructions, supplemented with working drawings, are the next best.

When a pair of snowshoes are to be made the first thing is to plan the size, shape and general character of the shoes. The frames, or bows, are the first step of the actual making.

Snowshoe frames are made of tough, light wood. Many kinds of wood are used, and while I am not prepared to say positively which kind is best I believe that young, straight grained white ash is about as good a wood as can be found. But my experience has been mostly with white birch, and my instructions for making the frames apply to the use of this wood in particular, for it is peculiar in many ways, and cannot be split and worked as freely as certain other kinds of wood.

To find a suitable tree for this purpose is sometimes difficult. I once went into the bush a distance of seven miles to get a tree which I had found, split it, and carried one half home. I surely earned that wood, but I made from it a pair of frames which were so light that old bushmen said I would break them on my first trip; however, I used them all winter, then gave them to an old German who wore them until the filling was completely gone, yet the frames were still good.

The tree from which the frames are to be made should be not more than eight inches in diameter, and one of six inches is better. It should have drooping branches, and must have eight or ten feet of the trunk straight and clean, free of limbs, and absolutely without a particle of twist to the grain. Such trees may be found occasionally growing along the edge of a swamp.

After the tree has been felled and a section of the proper length cut off, a groove about one and a half inches deep is carefully cut the entire length along one side, care being used not to strike hard, as that would injure the wood. When the groove is finished a similar one is cut on the opposite side. The stick should be split with wooden wedges, and if it is properly done the split will follow the grooves. The best half should then be chosen for the proposed snowshoe frames, and this should be ripped lengthwise with a saw, or split, as desired. Each of the pieces will make a frame or bow.

One side of the stick is then cut and planed until it is perfectly straight, and its face at a right angle to the bark side, or at least it must be so in the middle, which forms the toe of the snowshoe, for there should be nothing taken off the bark side, not even the bark, until after the wood is bent into shape for the snowshoe frame. It is best if the entire stick is worked out from the bark side, but the wood may be planed straight at all parts except in the middle, where the greatest strain comes. Then the

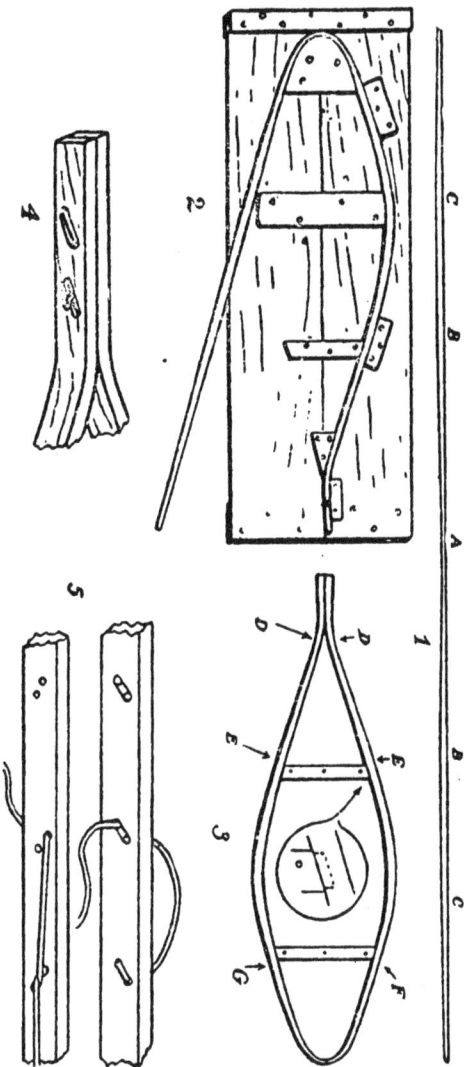

MAKING A SNOWSHOE FRAME. 1. THE STICK BEFORE BENDING. 2. BENDING ON THE FORM. 3. THE FINISHED FRAME. 4. THE END FASTENING. 5. THREADING THE LANYARD—INSIDE AND OUTSIDE OF FRAME.

third side of the stick is marked off with a marking gauge and either cut or sawed to the mark. The fourth side, the inside of the stick, which will be the inside of the finished frame, is then cut down to the proper dimensions, but on this side an even thickness is not maintained, the toe portion being cut thinnest, with the heel—ends of the stick—coming next. For a snowshoe of average size, say 44 inches in length and 14 inches wide, the stick should measure eight and a half feet in length, one inch in width, seven-eighths inch thick at the parts which will become the middle of the shoe (B to C in figure one), one-half inch at A, and about five-eighths inch at the ends.

Before anything more can be done with the wood a form for bending the frames must be made. A convenient form is shown in figure two. For steaming the wood properly it is necessary to have a steaming box, which is merely a long case made of narrow boards, open at both ends. The stick is placed in this case and the steam from a boiling tea kettle turned in one end so that the hot steam travels the entire length. The wood should be steamed thus an hour and then it is ready for bending.

Figure two shows how the wood is bent and secured on the form. The toe must be formed very carefully, bending only a little at first, then releasing, then bending a little more, and so on until the wood can be seasily and safely bent to complete shape and secured by nailing blocks to the form. The form should be made from two- inch planks, so that it will accommodate the two frames. The wood is allowed to dry thoroughly on the form before filling, and this will require at least two weeks.

After the frames are dry they may be taken from the form, the tail end of each fastened and the crossbars fitted into place. The ends may be secured with a wood screw until after the frames have been strung, but the screw should then be removed and the ends tied with rawhide, through gimlet holes, the part between being counter sunk so that the thongs will be protected from wear. This is shown in figure four.

The crossbars are pieces of flat, strong wood, about one and a fourth inches wide and nearly a half inch thick, with rounded edges. These should be placed about 16 or 17 inches apart, measuring from center to center, and so placed that when the frame is supended on the hands midway between these two sticks the tail will outweigh the toe by just a few ounces. These crossbars should be carefully mortised into the frame as shown in the small diagram in center of figure three.

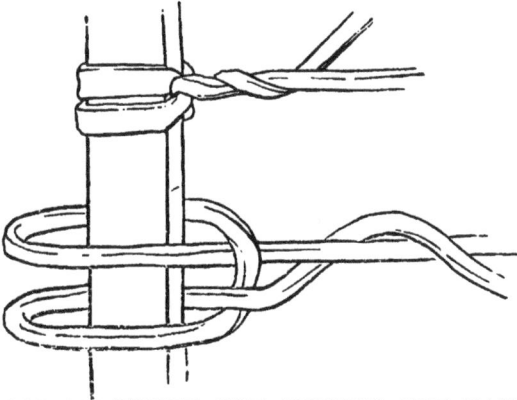

THE LOOP BY WHICH THE THONGS ARE FASTENED
TO THE FRAME.

In both sides of the frame from D to E, also from F to G, gimlet holes are bored through the bows from outside to inside at intervals of two inches, or a little more, the holes being in pairs obliquely placed, and countersunk between. Three holes are also bored through each crossbar, as shown.

The frames are now ready for filling. Regarding material for filling, for ordinary use, there is nothing equal to cowhide, a fairly heavy skin. The green hide should be placed under running water for a week or more, until the hair can be pulled out easily. The hair should then be pulled, or scraped off, but care must be used that the grain of the skin is not broken or scraped away. The hide should then be thoroughly stretched and dried in an airy but shady place. When dry it may be cut into strands. A whole hide will fill several pairs of shoes. The portion along the back is best and this should be used for filling the middle section. The lighter parts from the edges of the skin will answer for stringing the heels and toes. All strands should be cut lengthwise of the skin, and full length. Their width will depend on the thickness of the skin, the weight of filling desired in the snowshoe, the general character of the snow in which they will be used, and the size of mesh in the web. If cut while dry, then soaked, stretched, and again allowed to dry, as they will be when strung into the frames, it will be found that the length of the

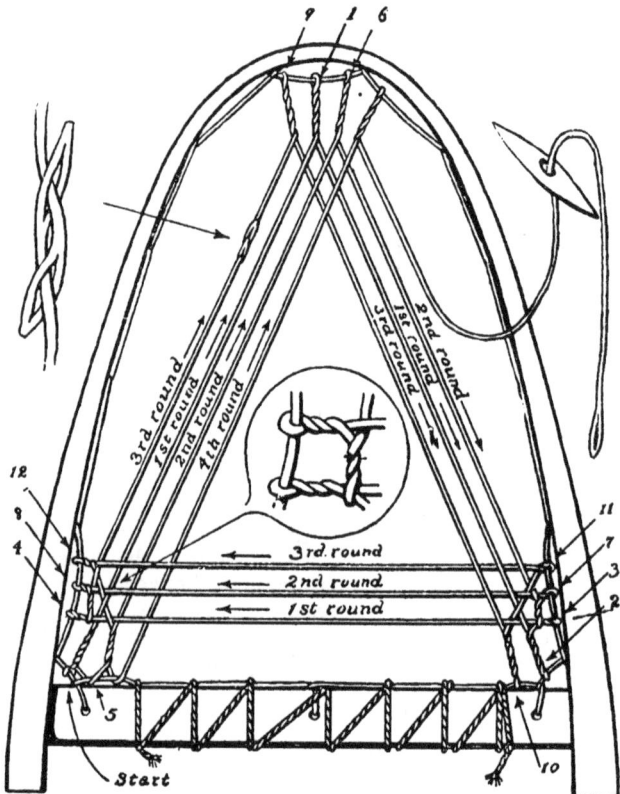

METHOD OF FILLING THE TOE SECTION.

strands will be increased greatly, while the thickness will be much
decreased. It is well to cut several trial widths, so that the
proper weight of strand may be determined. For a coarse
webbed shoe the thongs, after being stretched and dried, should
be about five-sixteenths of an inch wide for the middle portion
of the shoe; for the ends an eighth inch is sufficiently heavy.
These strands of hide should all be soaked and stretched thoroughly, allowed to dry while stretched, and then soaked again
just before using, and strung into the frames while wet.

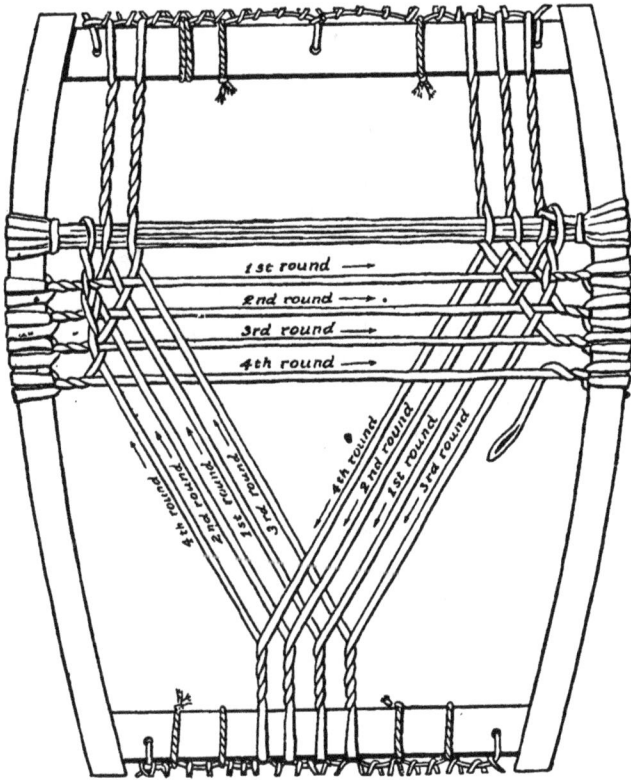

1st round →
2nd round →
3rd round →
4th round →

FILLING THE MIDDLE OF THE SNOWSHOE.

The ends are filled first and as I always commence with the toe I will describe my method of stringing that part first. A strand of the water-soaked rawhide is stretched tightly around the inside of the toe portion through the little gimlet holes, as shown in figure five, starting and finishing at one of the holes in the forward crossbar. This thong is called the lanyard, and its purpose is to hold the filling which is woven into the toe.

A small needle of very hard wood, or bone, is used for filling the ends. I have shown in the drawing how the filling runs. Starting in the lower left-hand corner it goes up to the part marked 1, passes around the lanyard, twists back around itself about an inch and then goes down to 2, there passing around the lanyard and again twisting around itself, then around the lanyard at 3, a single twist, and then across to 4, where it again turns around the lanyard, then twists down around the first strand to the starting point, under the lanyard at 5 and up to 6. From there the strand loops and twists the same as in the first round, except that at the lower corners it loops back around the first round, then twists around itself, then around the lanyard, and on the same as before. This looping back of every second round is continued until the filling extends across the entire forward part of the toe, when it is discontinued, and each round is made like the first. This looping back throws the filling alternately from side to side.

The filling must be stretched in very tightly and must not be allowed to slip. When one strand is used up another is joined on in the manner shown. Care must be used to see that every round crosses the others in the proper way, and all the twists must be made alike. The amateur should keep these pictures before him for a guide. Occasionally he should look his work over carefully, and if an error is discovered the stringing should be removed and made right. It will be necessary to straighten out the completed portions occasionally, and for this purpose I use a round-pointed hardwood stick. The weave will finish at the center of the crossbar.

The filling in the tail end or heel is very simple and is shown so plainly in the diagram that I think a description superfluous. It starts at the upper right-hand corner and finishes in the middle of the crossbar. I again advise that great care be used to get the twists and loops right, and to see that the thongs cross in the proper way.

Filling the middle section is also more simple than it appears at first glance, for it is practically a repetition of the system used in the toe portion. The edges of the wood should be rounded slightly to prevent them cutting the thongs. The Northern Indians wind this part of the frame with a strip of cloth, to make a sort of cushion for the tightly stretched thongs. This cloth winding serves its purpose well, but in a country where wet snows are common its use is not advised, for the cloth holds the dampness and causes the rawhide to rot.

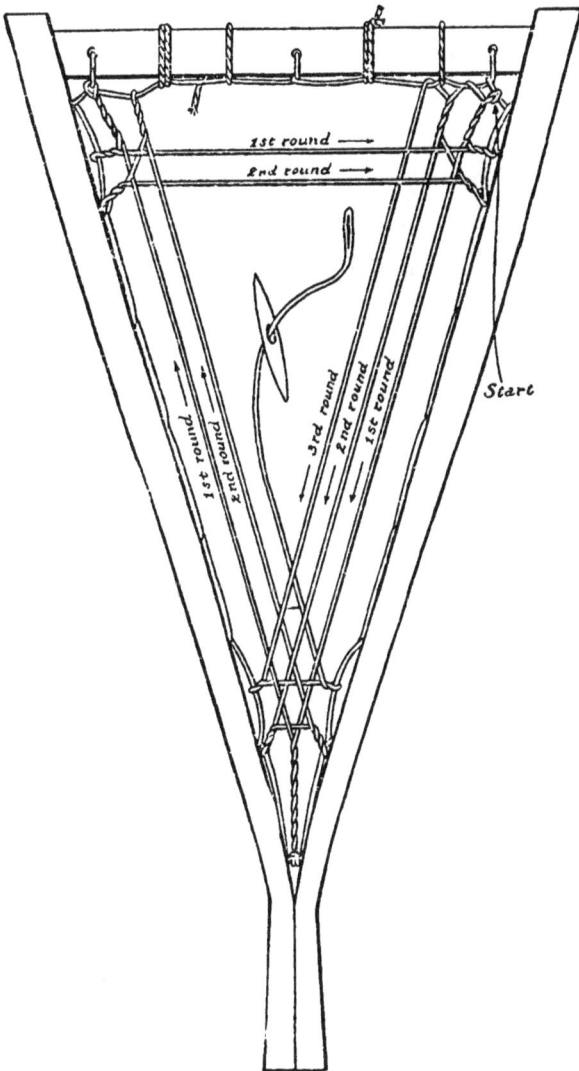

1st round →
2nd round →

Start

1st round
2nd round
3rd round
2nd round
1st round

HOW THE HEEL SECTION IS STRUNG.

While the system of stringing this part may appear quite intricate it is in reality simple, and it is the more elaborate arrangement of the forward portion that makes this section appear so complicated. The stout bunch of thongs shown in the drawing, known as the toe cord, is strung in first, the rawhide strand being tightly stretched and crossing the frame some four or five times, a loop being thrown around the whole on the inside of the frame on both sides in the last round. This should be so executed that the last loop will be on the right-hand side. The thong then loops around this bunch of cords again about an inch from the frame, from there being strung up around the crossbar, then twisting around itself back to the starting point, from there passing down diagonally to the center of the rear crossbar, where it loops and twists again, then up to the upper left-hand corner, where it twists up the same as on the opposite side. From here it will be noted the thong runs down a short distance and loops around the left side of the frame. The simple loop used for this purpose is clearly shown in a small drawing. From this loop the rawhide strand twists back about an inch, then runs straight across the shoe to the right, where the loop is repeated. This completes the first round of the filling. The second round starts in about the same way as the first, goes up to the crossbar at the left of the first round, twists back to the toe cord, from there to the rear crossbar, then up to the left-hand corner. Here the system changes, for the strand is run up and twisted around the toe cord and first round of filling before it is looped to the frame. After looping it is brought across to the right, where it again loops and twists, and then twists around the toe cord and first round of filling exactly as on the left, after which it is run down to the rear crossbar. In this way the stringing continues, every second round twisting forward around the preceding two. This binds the filling firmly and, it will be noted, also alternates the successive rounds from side to side. When the process of filling has progressed so far that there are four twists around the forward crossbar, on each side, this twisting should be stopped and the remainder of the forward portion left open, for this is where the foot of the wearer works through when walking. This open space should measure about four and a half inches in width, and if it does not the filling must be shifted. In very coarse meshed shoes three twists on each side will be all that can be given. An extra turn around the toe cord should also be made on each of these two twists of the filling, for considerable strain is thrown onto this portion. From this point on, instead of running forward and twisting around the crossbar, the filling simply twists around the toe cord. But here care must be used to keep the filling smooth and the toe cord flat, otherwise sore feet will result from wearing the shoes. The weave finishes in the center of the toe cord and there the end of the thong should be securely and neatly fastened. The last touch is to wind a strand of rawhide about the twisted thongs on each side of the foot opening and around the toe cord, to make these parts smooth and protect them from wear.

In the drawings of the heel and toe sections it will be noted that I have shown the web tied to the crossbars with twine. This is not a permanent feature, for when the center of the shoe has been filled these strings may be removed.

After making one pair of snowshoes the workman will undoubtedly see wherein he can improve on the design of the shoe, on the style of filling, or in the method of making. There are many labor-saving devices and ways of handling the material that make the work easier. But these the amateur snowshoe maker will learn in time and I believe I have now given all the instructions necessary for those who want to make their own snowshoes.

SNOWSHOES—HOW TO USE THEM

Snowshoes of one kind or another are used in all northern countries, for they are a necessity to those who live in the snowy north, and earn their living by outdoor work. Where or when they originated would be hard to say, definitely, but since it is in America that they have been perfected and were used by the Indians when this country was first visited by white men, it seems reasonable that the snowshoe is an invention of the early North American savages, and probably was first used many thousands of years ago.

The snowshoe is copied from one of Mother Nature's many unpatented inventions. She is the inventor of the snowshoe, for she gave this gift to many of the northern animals, for instance the marten, the snowshoe rabbit, and even the caribou. The marten and the rabbit have large heavily furred feet, especially large and furry during the winter, and because these feet cover a large area of snow in proportion to the animals' weight, they support their owners where animals unprovided with a "snowshoe" would sink, and would have great difficulty in traveling. The caribou has a highly split foot of large size; its spreads gives down under the animal's weight until the dew claws also help in supporting it, and thus cover so much surface that this big deer can walk on a snow crust that would not carry a man.

As a further illustration of nature's use of the snowshoe principle, compare the foot of a Canada lynx with that of a bobcat or bay lynx. The former animal, meant for an existence in the North and the high altitudes where deep snows prevail, has a very large, furry paw that supports the animal wonderfully on the loose snow, whereas the more southern wildcat, a very closely related species, has a foot relatively small and with shorter fur. The snowshoe therefore was merely copied from nature by mankind and no doubt it was a study of the natural animal snowshoe that gave the early-day savage the great idea and set him to work on a scheme by which he could increase the size of his feet in a convenient and practical manner, and thus be able to walk on the snow instead of wading through it.

Whatever may have been the style of the first snowshoes or the material used in them, the first white visitors to the American continent found the Indians using snowshoes with frames of wood, strung with rawhide, in fact, exactly the same as are being used to-day. While the white men may have sought to improve on materials and general form, it is certain that they could find nothing better or even as good, for the Indians' snowshoe was adopted and is being used in its original form to-day where serious use is required. Snowshoes are often modified in form for the use of the white people in and near the settlements, but for the rough, wild country the Indians' snowshoes cannot be surpassed, unless it be in the selection of materials and in workmanship.

Everybody knows that snow is not always of the same nature. The character of the snow depends on weather conditions. Cold weather causes it to remain loose and fluffy; warm days and cold nights settle the snow and form a crust, while during midday it becomes wet and packy; wind following a snowstorm makes drifts of more or less solidity. These are all very different conditions of snow and a snowshoe that is perfect in form for one kind of travel or one kind of snow cannot be per-

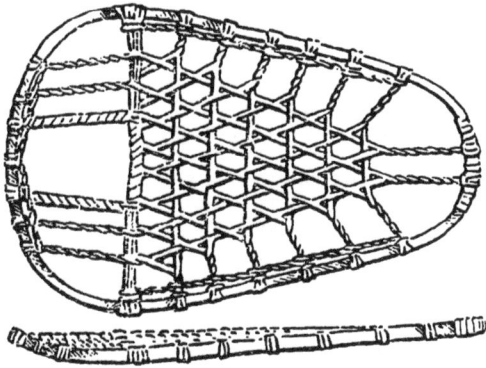

1

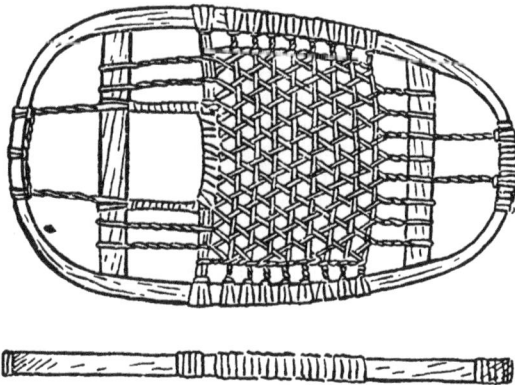

2

BEAR PAW SNOWSHOES. No. 1, WESTERN; No. 2, EASTERN.

fect for another, although it may answer for all kinds of use. In widely separated districts the prevailing weather conditions may cause one or another condition of snow to predominate the season through, and as a consequence the proper snowshoes to use in any particular place are the ones adapted to the prevailing snow conditions. Likewise the nature of the country with respect to surface and vegetation greatly influence the styles of snowshoes.

The sporting goods catalogues show snowshoes of very different forms and proportions, and the extreme conditions, not for general use. But the catalogues seldom give any information on this subject that will aid the tyro in selecting snowshoes adapted to his use, and if uninformed on the subject he is all at sea.

Long, narrow snowshoes are used for fast travel in open, fairly level country. In general, they are not good on rough ground, in brushy districts, or where the snow does not fall to a good depth. If the toes are turned up somewhat and more or less pointed they are better for travel in loose, powdery snow. But the upturned toes render the shoes worthless for hill climbing, as the frames will not take a grip on the snow, while on hard trails or crusted snow, such as we sometimes find on the frozen lakes, they make the wearer's feet sore through lack of spring in the frames.

The most perfect type of snowshoes for general use is that shown in figure five. It has the average dimensions and proportions, all extremes being avoided. It measures about 44 inches in length by 14 inches in width at the widest place, and this is the proper size for the average person and general conditions. A heavy man, if of average height, or taller, can use larger shoes to advantage, while for a smaller and lighter man slightly smaller snowshoes are better adapted. The toe is round and flat. It slips easily through the brush, takes a good grip on the hard snow of the hillsides and covers enough snow to keep it up near the surface while the narrow heel cuts down. The tail is short, which adapts the shoe better for turning in brushy places and reduces liability of breakage when crossing logs. The stringing, it will be noted, is heavy and coarse, which makes the shoe better for damp, sticky snow. A fine mesh filling is all right where the snow is always in a loose, dry condition, but when the snow becomes packy it closes up on the web and makes continuous trouble. The ends are filled with a finer material, for here the stringing is subject to less strain.

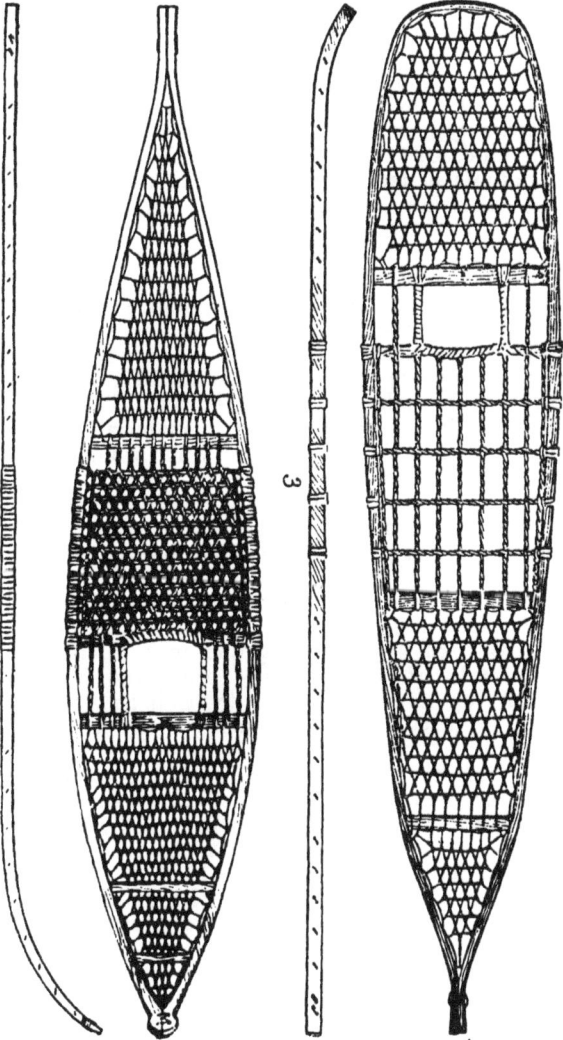

NORTHERN SNOWSHOES.
No. 3, ALASKA PATTERN; No. 4, THE CREE.

The Indians of Canada frequently fill the heel and toe of their snowshoes with fine twine instead of rawhide. This material wears much better than would be expected, providing the snow is deep and the snags well covered, as they are up there in winter. But a twine filling is not nearly as good as rawhide and is used only because it is a more convenient material.

Many kinds of raw skins are used for filling snowshoes, but there is nothing better than cowhide. Horsehide is said to wear very well. Calfskin is a good material for stringing light shoes, for use on broken trails or for women and children. Moose and caribou skin are much used in the North, but are not as durable as cowhide. Except that the hair is removed from the hide it undergoes no other preparation for snowshoe filling, no oiling nor tanning being permissible.

In the frames also various kinds of wood are used, this depending partly on the woods obtainable where the snowshoes are made. A tough, light wood is required. White men usually make use of white ash, a very good material for the purpose. Black ash is also used, but is a poor wood for snowshoe frames. The Canadian Indians use white and yellow birch, both very good if good judgment is used in selecting the trees. In the far Northwest snowshoe frames are sometimes made of spruce, while in the West service wood is frequently employed. There are many other woods that will answer very well.

In the illustration are shown two patterns of long, narrow snowshoes. One has a pointed, upturned toe, the frame being made in two pieces, fastened together with rawhide at heel and toe. This style of shoe I think originated in Northwestern Canada, anyway it is used there by Indians and whites alike. Snowshoes of this pattern are usually made five feet long and 12 inches wide. The toe curves up seven or eight inches and the length from the toe cords on which the wearer's foot rests to the point of the upturned toe must exceed the length from the ball of his foot to his knee; if it is not so, the toe of the snowshoe will strike his knee when he lifts his foot.

The other long pattern is a style used in Alaska and Yukon. It is so shaped that it gives the maximum of surface covering qualities for a shoe of that length and a practical width. The stringing is very open and is put into the frame by a peculiar system, quite unlike that used in other snowshoes. This is an excellent snowshoe for fast travel in deep, loose snow.

Very short snowshoes made without tails are known as the

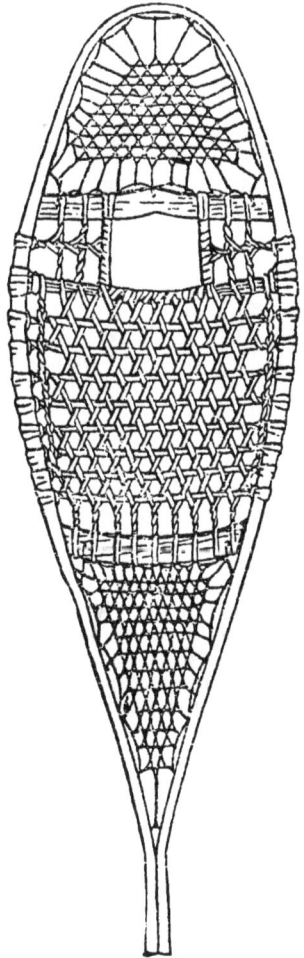

A SNOWSHOE OF STANDARD SHAPE, AND A FOOT HARNESS FOR SAME.

"bearpaw" pattern. I have shown two of these. The one made without crossbars is used by the Indians of Washington. It is a very simple, easily made snowshoe, and is especially useful in the rough, brushy ground. It works nicely in the mountains of Pennsylvania and is probably as good for use in that place as in the Northwest. The other bearpaw shoe illustrated is a style that originated in the Adirondack Mountains. It was designed for the use of the spruce gum hunters, its short length making it a perfect snowshoe for use in gumming, walking around trees, turning and zigzagging here and there. This pattern is one of the best for very brushy ground, where rocks and fallen trees abound, and it is the best shape for use in the North when the first snows come and the small underbrush, snags, rocks and logs are not yet deeply buried. A pair of snowshoes like this may be carried in a packsack if the trapper is making a journey over his line when the first deep snow is due, and he will not then be caught without snowshoes when a day's journey or two from camp. This has happened to me, so I can now see the importance of carrying a pair of snowshoes at that time.

Snowshoes of all types have an opening in the forward part of the central section through which the wearer's toes move as he walks. At the rear edge of this opening are the toe cords, a bunch of five or six strands of rawhide, and when in use this part is beneath the ball of the foot. A toe-strap passes over the foot at this point. There is always some other form of fastening used, but this may be anything from the Indian's hitch of soft caribou skin or lamp wicking to the harness leather fastening of the white man, which buckles across the instep and above the heel. In all cases the fastening must pass around the foot above the heel, for it is this strap that supports the weight of the snowshoe as the foot is lifted; it is moved forward by the toe strap, and this piece also holds the foot in place on the shoe.

The Indian's method of tying a snowshoe to the foot has some advantages over the white man's harness fastening, but in other ways it is imperfect. The principal advantage is that the fastening need not be opened for removing the snowshoes or attaching it. I have used snowshoes a week at a time without opening the knot. A simple twist of the foot with bended knee will serve to free the snowshoe from the foot and it is just as easily replaced. But it does not hold the shoe as rigidly with respect to side motion as the strap and buckle adopted by white men generally, and I think it is more likely to cause soreness of the feet. The harness shown is one of the best styles and is easily made and adjusted.

For snowshoeing in Northern districts, where the weather is cold all through the winter and the snow remains in a loose, dry condition, buckskin moccasins are the best footwear. By this I mean moccasins of any kind of deerskin, tanned by the Indian method. Such moccasins are not waterproof, but that makes little difference, for the dry snow never makes wet feet. Buckskin is soft and light and if the moccasins are large, plenty of warm, woolen socks may be worn. For spring wear, when the snow is more or less damp, or for use anywhere when the snow is in this condition, oil tanned moccasins or rubber overshoes may be worn. Rubber is somewhat hard on the filling of the snowshoes, but if this is heavy and of good material it will stand a lot of wear. Ordinary rubber shoes should not be worn, however, without first removing the heels.

When walking the entire snowshoe is never lifted clear of the snow; the tail always drags. It is easy to learn to use them. I walked 12 miles the first day I tried snowshoeing. My greatest trouble was in keeping one shoe clear of the other, but this is soon learned. There may also be trouble in learning to turn, especially in brushy places, and in attempting to cross logs. When crossing a log the foot itself must be placed on the log and the next step must be of sufficient length for the snowshoe to clear it, or the foot must be turned sideways.

To get satisfactory service from a pair of snowshoes necessitates proper care. The wearer should always avoid walking over snags, or little hummocks, which are certain indications of objects barely covered and which may injure the web of the shoes. Do not step on a place which will support one or both ends of the shoe solidly unless the middle portion is also thus supported, for if the frames do not break the strain they will be weakened and will sooner or later take on a curved shape. Never step down from a high place with all of your weight on the snowshoes, for the strain on filling and frame is great.

Snowshoes require care, not only while in use, but at other times as well. Being strung with rawhide, this material is very susceptible to heat and moisture. If the shoes are not dried thoroughly after becoming damp or wet the stringing will rot, while if dried too rapidly the filling becomes brittle and breaks when put to a strain. In camp snowshoes should be suspended from the ceiling by a wire, for mice will eat the filling if they can reach them. Shoes should be watched closely also for worn strands and when a string looks dangerously weak the shoe should be repaired at once.

It cannot be expected that after the most exhaustive book study the novice will know enough about snowshoes to discriminate between the ordinary bad and those without fault. But there are points that if kept in mind will aid greatly in selecting snowshoes that will not only be desirable, but also satisfactory in regard to size, proportions and pattern. The extreme styles, as already pointed out, are not for the use of the beginner, for his snowshoeing is generally of the regulation kind. The snowshoes which he should buy, and which he will find in stock with most dealers, are more or less on the lines of the pattern shown in figure 5. The standard size, or about 14x44 inches, will answer well in nearly all cases. If the country is not too rough and hilly they may have the toes turned up an inch or two, but otherwise they should be flat, as shown. It matters little whether the toe be round, square or quite pointed, but it should be rather large in area while the heel end should be narrow. The long tail usually found on stock snowshoes is a nuisance and may as a rule be cut off to advantage, for usually the balance of the snowshoe is improved by so doing.

A snowshoe should almost balance when suspended midway between the two cross-bars, the tail end being just a little the heavier. Very few stock snowshoes are so made, most of them being too heavy in the rear.

When buying snowshoes examine the frames with care, for if they are not made of good, straight grained wood they are apt to break. The wood should be heaviest at the sides and thinnest at the toe. There must be no knots, cuts or other defects. Sometimes in bending the frames the makers split slivers loose and afterwards glue them down, so look carefully for such places.

The filling should be clear and yellow. It should be of almost equal thickness and there should be no splices close to the frame or in the centre. See that the thongs are thoroughly stretched, for poorly stretched filling is sure to stretch and sag the first time the shoes are used on damp snow. If the thongs do not run perfectly straight across the shoe, reject it, for this is a sure sign of poorly stretched filling.

What are sold as first-class snowshoes bring prices ranging roughly from five to ten dollars per pair. Good snowshoes can-

not be made and sold at less than five dollars, and if they are
large or have much work about them they cannot be made for
this price. I do not find any material difference between snowshoes of Indian make and those made by white men. The very
best snowshoes I have ever found being made for sale are those
made by a friend of mine living in the Adirondacks. He uses the
best of material throughout and the stringing alone used in a
pair of his best shoes will cost him as much as the price at which
oridinary snowshoes are sold. The best possible snowshoes are
not available to many readers of this article unless they have
learned to make them, in which case they can use as much care
and as good material as desired.

WINTER TRAVEL IN THE WOODS

What a change comes over the great forests of the North
when winter reigns and holds all nature in his icy grip. The
fleecy mantle of white covers hill and vale, stream and bush
alike, bending to the ground the lower branches of the spruces
and hemlocks, smoothing over the rough trails of the fall, and
burying the logs, stumps and underbrush from view until the following spring. The woods through which we traveled with ease
and comfort when the ground was bare now has a forbidding
appearance and it requires all the nerve we can muster to attempt
to penetrate the dense, snow-laden growth, where we know that
the first step will release a small avalanche of snow upon us. The
bended branches and smaller growths of the thickets give a different appearance to the woods and distances seem shorter so
that we find it difficult to keep to the old course, and wise is the
trapper or other woods traveler who has blazed out his main
trails before the coming of the snow. In this winter woods it
would seem that only the wild creatures inhabiting it would be at
home and perfectly familiar with the changed surroundings.

But the seasoned woodsman does not hesitate to travel the
winter trail. If he is a trapper or spruce gummer the winter is
his harvest time. He feels little of the storms which in more
exposed country would keep one close indoors much of the time.
On a still morning the cold may be intense and on all sides will
be heard pistol-like reports from the freezing trees, but if he
cannot keep warm by rapid walking, he treads down a spot of
snow, pulls some loose bark from a white birch tree, places over

it dead branches broken from the trunk of a nearby evergreen and applies a lighted match to the oily birch bark. In a few seconds he has a roaring fire by the side of which he can rest and restore the chilled blood to its normal state. The Northern frost gives no warning; it creeps cautiously through the clothing and at once commences to freeze the flesh beneath and at such times a fire cannot be lighted too quickly.

One cannot travel the snowy bush in comfort and safety unless he wisely prepares for such travel, by wearing the proper clothing and carrying with him the most suitable equipment. Clothing must be of the correct weight; just heavy enough to keep the wearer warm while traveling but no heavier, as bulky clothing is tiresome to one who walks the trails. A long coat is bad for travel; it clings to the legs and interferes with stepping over logs. The outer clothing should be of a kind to which the snow will not cling, yet it must be soft. Wind proof cloth is not needed, in fact a medium thick but loosely woven cloth is warmer in the woods than smooth, closely woven fabrics. The vest or waist coat is seldom worn in the forest, at least not by woodsmen. Woolen clothing, always, is the choice.

What I know on this subject I have learned from actual experience, and we are told that experience is the best teacher, but we could often save ourselves much discomfort if we would profit by the advice of others. However, knowledge acquired at the expense of time, health, comfort and money is often less costly than ignorance. The clothing and outfits I recommend are those I have found best for my own use, but an article is most useful when properly used.

I consider the following the best dress for winter wear in the timbered country of the North and so dressed a healthy man may travel the wintry woods in comfort. Starting with underwear, I advise wearing pure woolen goods, always, of medium weight, and all in one piece. The soft, fine kind should be chosen.

THE WINTER TRAIL.

Wool absorbs the perspiration and is reasonably warm when damp or even wet. It never gets cold and uncomfortable like cotton underwear does, the nap does not flatten down, and it keeps the skin warm and induces a healthy circulation of the blood near the surface.

Wear woolen socks for the same reasons; two or three pairs, as required, and a pair of heavy knit wool stockings, knee length, over them. This is too much for warm weather, but I am talking of clothing for wear when it is cold. The amount of stock-

THE WINTER TRAIL.

ings required will depend somewhat on the constitution of the man who wears them; for one traveler can keep the feet warm with what would not be sufficient for another. Do not at any time wear more socks than necessary, and wash them frequently, as it freshens the wool and makes them warmer. A number of pairs of medium weight socks are better than one pair of very heavy ones. They are easier washed, easier dried and more comfortable. Many bushmen wind a strip of woolen blanket about the foot, and this has the advantage of being cheaper than extra socks. I wear both the socks and the long stockings on the outside of the trousers, and the stockings should be held by a strap at the top. Stretch out the toes of the socks and stockings a little before putting the shoes or moccasins on over them and it will keep them from binding the toes.

The only footwear for winter travel when the weather is cold, especially for snowshoeing, is the buckskin moccasin. By "buckskin" I mean Indian tanned moosehide, deer or caribou skin, or the white man's asbestol cordovan horsehide, the latter being the best wearing material, but not as soft and comfortable as the others. Caribou skin moccasins are my preference for snowshoeing, and I like the Ojibway pattern with pointed toe and cloth top; they are not as likely to cause sore toes as the Sioux pattern (the regular factory made style) and the cloth top is warm and holds the snowshoe strings better than the buckskin top does.

Buckskin moccasins are not waterproof, in fact water will go through them almost as readily as through cloth, but waterproof qualities are not required in footwear for winter use in the North, as the snow never becomes damp until spring, and all water, except the smooth rapids, is well covered with ice. The only time when the traveler is likely to get wet feet is when snowshoeing over the ice on the lakes; then after a wind storm there is sure to be water under the snow on the ice.

A medium weight gray woolen shirt suits me best for woods wear. Trousers may be of almost any kind of strong, soft woolen material, and should be roomy, but fit well at the waist. I prefer to wear a belt rather than suspenders, but this is immaterial. If the snow clings to the trousers behind the knees, when snowshoeing, wear light overalls over them. I have never found anything better in coats than those made of mackinaw cloth, such as lumbermen wear. I like the plain colors best, blue black being my choice. All outside pockets should be covered with flaps to keep the snow out. Mackinaw is a soft, warm material and it will turn considerable rain. It has only one objectionable feature —the snow will cling to it, especially across one's back just above the pack sack, which the woodsman nearly always has with him; the warmth coming through the cloth causes it to collect the snow.

My choice of head dress is a good grade, long wool toque which can be drawn down over the forehead and ears. Over this I sometimes wear a sort of hood made of thin woolen cloth, which hangs down well over the collar of the coat and ties under the chin. This hood is very desirable, as it is a great protection from cold and snow. When walking through a snow-laden evergreen bush there is a constant shower of snow being released from the boughs and this hood keeps the falling snow from getting inside of the clothing, which it surely would do without this protection. It is also a shield against the cold wind when crossing frozen lakes, where the toque alone would not give sufficient protection. I steer clear of fur caps. They are too warm for walking, and I think it best to have no covering over the face, as any such arrangement will gather moisture from the breath and cause freezing. Unless one is exposed to a severe wind, holding the mittened hands against the face occasionally will prevent freezing in the coldest weather, providing we do not have to face the breeze.

The hands also need special protection from the cold and much could be written on this subject. I know of nothing better than mittens, not gloves, made of heavy woolen cloth, with a pair of cotton ones drawn over them. They are easier dried than a single pair of heavy ones; are easily made from old material, costing nothing, and are warm. They should be loose enough to pull off quickly, and the tops should come well up over the wrists inside the coat sleeves. Do not buy gauntlet gloves for the woods; they collect dirt and snow continually. No kind of leather gloves or mittens that I have ever worn will keep my hands warm unless they are very heavily lined and then they are stiff, so I prefer the cloth ones.

So much for cold weather clothing, but what shall we wear when the sun commences to travel his northern trail and the grip of Jack Frost weakens; when the snow melts during midday and our clothing seems uncomfortably warm. At such times we can discard the heavy shirt and substitute a lighter one; leave the overalls in camp and put the hood in the pack or the coat pocket, and wear fewer socks, with oil-tanned shoe pacs instead of buckskin moccasins. They are not as good for snowshoeing, but are waterproof if kept well oiled. Rubber shoes wear the filling of the snowshoe badly.

While I have been speaking of clothing for wear in the timbered districts of the Far North I realize that there are more of those who read this living in a less frosty climate, but for all of the Northern States this clothing is quite suitable and proper, with the exception of the hood and moccasins. The former is seldom needed in more open hardwood forest, and as snowshoes are not used much the shoe pac and rubber shoe are the footwear

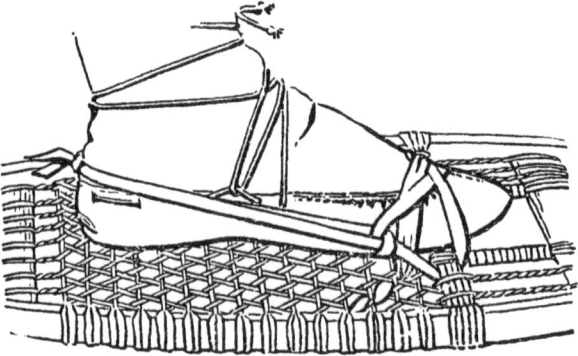

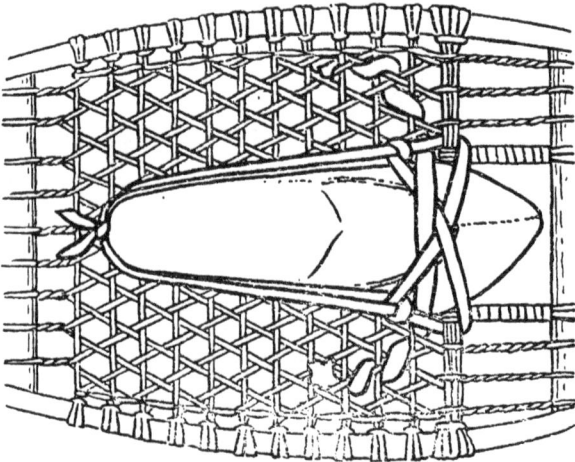

THE INDIAN SNOWSHOE HITCH.

most often seen. For walking on bare ground or in shallow snow, both shoes have advantages and faults. The rubbers are heavier than the pacs and more protection to tender feet, but are more likely to tire the wearer, especially since rubber clings so fondly to all brush and weeds with which it comes in contact.

But the pacs, while lighter and softer, will make tender feet sore on the bottoms, and they slip in snow more than do rubbers. My favorite rubber shoes for outdoor wear are those of ankle height, fastening with a lace or with strap and buckle.

Snowshoes can hardly be considered wearing apparel. An Italian who came over to Canada, when cold weather came, began to inquire about clothing for wear in that climate. When he asked what kind of footwear was best his informant told him that he thought snowshoes were the best when the snow came. Having no idea what snowshoes were he went to a store and asked to be shown some, and he was considerably surprised when he saw what they were. Snowshoes, however, are a part of the Northern woodsman's equipment, and a very necessary part. They are offered in a number of patterns by sporting goods dealers, and there are other styles made and used that are seldom or never seen in stores. Some are good; others are better, but each kind is good in some section of the country. It is not my object to go into detail in describing snowshoes, but I feel that I must say something about the patterns best adapted for use in the woods. They should be of about the standard shape, either round or square toe, as desired; for the average man, about 14 by 48 inches in size; frames of good straight grained wood, with the crossbars mortised in without weakening the bows. The tail should be fastened with rawhide, counter-sunk, and not a screw or rivet; and the filling throughout should be of good rawhide thoroughly stretched, rather fine and close in the ends and coarse and open in the centers. The toe should be large and quite broad, the tail narrow, and they should balance at a point just a few inches behind the center of the space between the crossbars. With such shoes you can travel fast on loose snow or hard; they turn easily; the broad flat toe takes a good grip and makes hill climbing easy, and it also stays nearly on the surface of the snow while the narrow tail cuts down and as a consequence they lift easily for the next step. If the filling is too close in the center the snow will pack under the foot; if the toes are too small they cut down and loose snow falls on top, making them heavy to lift; if the tail is too heavy it is difficult to turn with them; if the toe is upturned they slip on a crust or hard trail, make the feet sore, and are not good for climbing hills. Unless you know just what you are doing it is a good rule to avoid extreme styles.

If you are a "Down East" man you will undoubtedly select

some kind of snowshoe boot, harness, fastening or whatever you choose to call it. Most of these give satisfaction, but I have used the Indians' method mostly, the same being a tie or hitch with a piece of five-eighth-inch lamp wick, about four feet long. The toe strap is separate and is fastened by weaving the ends in and out of the filling at the sides of the toe opening. The way of tying to the foot is shown in the illustration more plainly than I can describe it. Both strings are tied together above the heel, and when properly adjusted it is not necessary to untie for putting the shoe on or removing it from the foot; a simple twist will do it. I have used snowshoes for a week or more without undoing the fastening, and it is very nice in extreme cold weather to be able to put on or remove shoes without baring the hands.

If you are simply traveling through the woods aimlessly, with no intention of making future use of the trail, it makes little difference how you go, but if you are a trapper and are breaking out a trap line you will, of course, aim to strike the good places for sets without walking farther than necessary, and you should make your trail with a view of using it afterwards, avoiding steep ascents and dense thickets. If possible, get over your trail the second time before the packed snow hardens and the trail will be smoother. Blaze your trail on trees and brush as you go along. I think it best to mark the brush by cutting them half off and bending them away from the trail. If you must mark trees, mark two sides and then you can follow the marks either way, and you can also indicate the turns in the path. My objection to marks on trees are that they cannot be seen as plainly as cut brush, especially after a driving snowstorm, when the snow clings to the trunks of trees, and that the drooping, snow-laden branches often hide the spots just when you need to see them most. A foot of fresh fallen snow may completely obliterate your trail, but if it is well marked you can follow it still, and the beaten bottom makes easier traveling, no difference how much snow has fallen over it.

Breaking out fresh trails is hard work, and slow. You can break trail away from camp six hours, and return over the broken trail in two. In a snowy climate it is advisable, whenever possible, to travel each permanent trail at least once in ten days to keep it in good condition; but the trapper will want to get over the ground oftener than that anyway.

As snowshoes are costly and their life depends much on the care they receive I will give some rules covering this point that is always well to observe. In breaking out a fresh trail avoid snags which show through the snow or little protuberances which indicate snags beneath the surface; also beware of places where the snow appears to be held up by brush or sticks beneath. I once broke a new snowshoe frame by stepping into a concealed hole; the whole trail dropped down and my snowshoe caught on a snag of a nearby stump, breaking a section out of the frame. It is the stringing, however, that is usually cut out by the snags. Be careful also when crossing logs to see that the shoes are not supported solidly at the ends while the middle is free to go down; such treatment will either break the frames or bend and strain them, and if they assume a curved shape they are unsightly and tiring to the feet, also hard to use in hill climbing. I always like to get started on the trail as early in the morning as possible, so that I can travel a few miles before daylight, and I camp early in the evening so I can get wood and make a comfortable camp before dark. In the early spring, when the snow melts during the day and clings to the snowshoes the only time one can travel is in the morning until about ten o'clock, and late in the evening. At night, if the moon shines, one can make good time, but through the day is the best time for resting at this season. When the snow sticks, the snowshoes get wet and heavy and damp snow packs on top and clings to them, and when these troubles come it is best to cut wood, build a good fire and camp by it until evening. Stand the snowshoes up in the snow where the sunshine and the warm wind will dry them, make some tea and eat your lunch, then roll into your blanket and rest until the sun gets low, when you can resume your journey.

It is difficult traveling, at the best, and the strength of the traveler is heavily taxed. Always he has the heavy pack and the snowshoe trail seems endless. The home camp is ever a welcome sight. It means greater comfort and usually a day of rest to wash and mend the clothing, and admire the drying furs, the harvest of the traps. There are days of awful cold, and the deep, loose snow seems almost too much to endure; yet with all the hardships and privations there is an inexplainable fascination connected with the free, wild life in the woods and in tramping the winter trail.

TRAVELING IN THE PATH-LESS WOODS

PART I.

Everybody admires the man who can travel in the woods without getting lost. Such a man always commands respect among his less accomplished associates. The sportsman never ceases to wonder at the ability of his guide to find his way unfailingly through the dense bush, and the white guide also admires and wonders at the Indian's accomplishments in the same line. To the uninitiated the feats of the woodsman seem like a sixth sense—instinct, they call it. But it is not instinct, but simply the application of knowledge which comes to those who are forced by circumstances to be observing in such matters. The man who can take an outfit on his back and travel a month in the wilderness, living without a particle of aid from his fellow men, is a woodsman, and he possesses a knowledge of woodcraft which would make a better world if it could be imparted to all mankind.

I was born and grew to manhood in one of the wildest and roughest districts of Pennsylvania. Northeast from my home I could travel 30 miles without seeing a human habitation, and northward the wild, uninhabited mountains reached a like distance, broken at one place only by a narrow valley in which there were a few small farms. Little by little I learned to know these mountains and the narrow valleys between. There was not a stream within 10 or 15 miles where I had not fished for trout and trapped for mink and 'coons, and I had hunted every swamp and red brush flat for deer, bears and grouse. I knew every place where blueberries grew in sufficient numbers to make the gathering profitable, and often I wandered long distances merely for the pleasure of mountain travel. I soon got the reputation of being an accomplished woodsman, an honor which I did not deserve, for I knew nothing whatever about travel in real wilderness. The long mountains paralleling one another made it easy to get about without losing the sense of direction, and I kept my compass points merely by familiarity with the ground on which I traveled.

When at the age of 23 I went into the wilderness of Canada, I was up against an entirely different proposition. Before me were hundreds of miles of unbroken bush, spotted with lakes that at first looked all alike to me, and cut by small streams which

A COMPASS OF A PRACTICAL TYPE.

flowed about from lake to lake in the most haphazard fashion imaginable. I had never traveled with the sun as a guide and knew nothing regarding the use of a compass, both of which are essential for wilderness travel.

My first move was to file on a piece of government land. The land guide helped to locate me and while we were looking about I saw him look at his compass, then he remarked that it was just noon and we would make some tea. I was surprised to see him get the time of day from a compass and asked him how he knew it was noon. "Because the sun is directly south," he answered, "and it is in that position only at noon." And then he explained to me how a compass could be used as a watch, with fair accuracy, and how a watch could be made to answer very well as a compass.

The woodsman told me that I could not travel in that country without a compass, and I soon found that such was the case. I borrowed a compass from a friend, a small, slip-cover instrument with a stop to hold the needle stationary when not in use. But I found that the slip-cover was inconvenient; dust got in at the stop opening and hampered the movement of the needle; and finally the compass slipped through a hole in my pocket and was lost. By these experiences I learned that the most practical form of compass for a woodsman was an open-face, watch-shaped instrument, without a stop, and with a ring by which it could be fastened to the coat or vest like a watch. Such an instrument does not have the long life of the finer stop compass, but it costs only a dollar or thereabouts, and after a year or two of use can be thrown away and a new one purchased. Of course, if a stop compass can be found that has no outside opening to admit dust it is better still.

An Indian seldom carries a compass, but he travels mainly by the "lay of the land." He learns the country just as I learned the mountains of Pennsylvania, and as a rule he has little idea of direction. Sometimes he travels by sun, in fact the sun answers for both watch and compass. But when the sun is invisible and the ground unfamiliar he sometimes meets with trouble and "loses his wigwam." But he is much less apt to get lost than a white man, under similar conditions, for when he loses his bearings he doesn't lose his head, in fact he doesn't consider it a serious matter at all. He simply makes camp and the next day he travels on until he rights himself again. The Indian also, when forced to it, uses means of getting his bearings which only Indians and veteran woodsmen know how to use.

For my own part I travel mostly by the sun when on strange ground, verifying my directions occasionally by reference to the compass. I also study landmarks and make use of them constantly, for to travel by compass alone is slow and difficult.

Comparatively few people who have never used a compass know how the instrument works; indeed, I once knew a man who thought that the needle pointed towards home when the owner lost his bearings. But it doesn't do any such thing unless by chance the home lies north.

On the peninsula of Boothia Felix, which juts into the Arctic Sea northwest of Hudson's Bay, is the magnetic north pole, and the needle of the compass, when free to revolve, points to this particular part of the earth. It does not point directly towards the magnetic pole in all parts of the world, for the magnetic currents which converge there do not flow in straight lines. In fact, there is an area in Asia, where the compass needle is deflected and points to a smaller local magnetic pole. But for bush travel all that is necessary is to consider that the blue end of the compass needle points north, and to call this point north always, the opposite direction, of course, being south.

Perhaps I should not say that the needle always points north, for it may lose its magnetism with age or the pivot on which it swings may become dulled, or again the needle may be deflected by a metal object being brought too near. If the needle behaves queerly, maybe you are holding it too near your gun, or some metal object in your belt or pocket may be attracting it. All objects of iron or steel become magnetized to a certain extent and will attract the needle if brought too near. But aside from such outside influence, and that of wear, the compass is a perfectly reliable instrument. Sometimes it tells us that the sun rises in the northwest, in which case we should believe it without question, for if we go contrary to the teachings of the instrument we will find that 99 times out of 100 the compass is right and we are dead wrong. One of the greatest mistakes a man can make when he gets turned around in the big timber is to doubt his compass, but many people will take a chance on their very unreliable instinct rather than to trust a perfectly trustworthy instrument which was brought into the woods to serve them on just such occasions. But one need never be in doubt, for if the needle swings freely and settles down in the same position each time, he may be sure that the instrument is all right.

By referring to the drawing, which shows a very common type of compass, it will be noted that the dial is graduated in degrees, on its outer edge, with the principal points marked with letters. These letters mean north, east, south, west, northeast, southeast, etc. To make the compass work perfectly it must be held level and steady until the needle stops swinging, then the compass can be turned easily, so that the blue end of the needle stands over the letter "N." When this is done all the points of the compass are shown. The only way a compass can be used is to show these directions, and, of course, the user should know which way he wants to go. Usually a man in the woods knows some familiar landmark; it may be a stream, a lake, a mountain, or even the railroad which he left when he entered the woods, and he will know whether he is north, south, east or west of this landmark, so there is little excuse for getting completely lost.

A ROUTE TRAVELLED BY COMPASS.

But if he is so hopelessly muddled that he doesn't know for the life of him whether he is in the Grand Canyon or a Canadian swamp the compass will not help him very much. If he is traveling north of his landmark he can return to it by going south, and the compass will tell him quickly which direction is south.

Suppose you have made a camp in the wilds and have set out to explore the surrounding country. For the sake of illustration I have drawn a map of some of my old-time hunting ground, showing the location of one of my camps. The first move would be to learn the country in the immediate vicinity of camp. The stream by the side of the camp flows east and this would be the first with which to get acquainted. A trip along the stream both ways from camp will serve to familiarize one with the stream and nearby country, so that he would have a good landmark, and he could hardly cross this stream knowing that it was the same one which flows by the camp. He would also know, if he were to reach this creek, whether the camp lay up stream or down. This then would serve as a base from which to operate. We will say now that he wishes to see some of the country north and northwest of camp. He sees in the distance a high hill with a peculiar bunch of trees on its summit. By referring to the compass he finds that the position of this hill is a little east of north. Then facing in that direction he notes that the sun is behind his right shoulder, for it is morning and the sun is in the southeast. Replacing the compass in his pocket he starts toward the tree-crowned hill which he has chosen as an objective point. As long as the hill is in sight he has clear sailing, but when the forest hides his landmark from view he keeps traveling straight ahead, maintaining his same position with reference to the sun. But the sun is also moving and he dare not go far without again looking at the compass and noting the changed position of the sun. This, you will see, is traveling by landmark. by compass, and by sun, and it will be found a very practical way.

But a man cannot travel straight in the average wilderness country, for nature imposes obstacles. Lakes, swamps, unfordable streams and other natural obstructions force detours, all of which must be kept in mind and a general straight course maintained.

Presuming that in spite of the unavoidable detours the traveler has kept a reasonable straight course and has reached the high hill with its peculiar clump of trees, he will know now that since his course has been a little east of north his camp must be just that much west of south from this hill. It would be an easy matter for him to retrace his steps to camp if he wished to do so.

From the top of the hill the explorer studies the topography of the surrounding country, and notes the lakes; the hollows, which indicate water courses; the swamp and clump of evergreen bush. Perhaps he sketches a map of what he sees, the details to be added as the country is learned more thoroughly.

To the northwest he sees what appears to be a fairly large lake, and as this looks interesting he sets out in that direction, traveling as before, by sun, compass and marker. Sometimes he can pick a mark a half mile distant and at other times he must be content to make use of a dead tree standing a hundred yards or less away. But near or far, they all serve the same purpose.

Having reached his objective he finds that what appeared to be a large lake is in reality a chain of small lakes or ponds and he draws them into his map.

Then he sets out down stream, noting that it flows in a southwesterly direction, and occasionally he takes a compass bearing to make sure that this course has not changed. After traveling about a mile he decides to return to camp. By carefully considering the distance traveled in each direction he concludes that he is now about two and a half miles northwest of camp, therefore he must travel southeast, so he starts in that direction. When about a quarter of a mile from camp he recognizes the surroundings and changes his course a little at the point marked by the arrow, and goes straight to camp.

In the same way the camper would explore the country for a few miles east, west and south, and when he has become reasonably well acquainted with this ground he is ready to push his explorations to greater distance, knowing that he can without difficulty return to familiar ground, and then easily find his camp, for he could not cross the section of country with which he is now familiar without recognizing it.

TRAVELING IN THE PATH-LESS WOODS

Part II.

To travel in a straight line by compass, and to keep your bearings regardless of how or where you go, is easy, if the rules I have given are followed; but people do not always know these rules, or for one reason or another they do not observe them. As a result they get lost. What to do in such a case I can't tell; but one thing that should not be done is to get frightened and travel desperately first in one direction, then in another, always more or less in circles, as men do when they wander aimlessly.

I am a firm believer in that "ounce of prevention" adage, for prevention is better than cure every time. This policy has carried me through hundreds of miles of wilderness without once getting lost. I have never been lost, although many times I have lost my bearings for awhile when traveling in company with somebody who was leading the way, or when trying to travel in unfamiliar country without using the methods I have been describing. I have never gone astray when using a compass, or when traveling by any of the other ways I have mentioned.

A short time ago I was talking about bush travel with a friend and after he had listened to my chatter for awhile he asked, "What would you do if you were to get lost?" "I wouldn't get lost," I answered, "for the rules I have been explaining to you are to prevent that and will always do so if followed. I always follow them." "That sounds all right," he argued, "but you know people do get lost sometimes and I want to know what a man should do if he gets lost. You say that you first get acquainted with the country near camp, then explore farther, etc., but here now is something different. I go into the woods to hunt deer, with a few fellows. We know nothing of the country and are dependent on our guides. They have led us into camp and we scarcely know how we came. Well, the next day, I set out to look for game, alone, intending to hunt close to camp. I go first this way and then that way, looking at the likely places, and after awhile it dawns on me that I don't know which direction to go to reach camp. In other words, I am lost. Now what should I do?" I will confess that the question was too much for me. Having never been lost, I had no experience of this kind from which to draw. I recalled stories of people who were lost but couldn't think of anything that would help a lost man find his way. There are many ways to find the compass points, but when a man doesn't know what direction he wants to travel, what good is there in knowing which is north and east?

I suggested to my friend that a man would surely always have some point in mind with which he was acquainted and would know approximately which direction this place lay. "If he does he isn't lost," he replied. "And even if he knows that the railroad runs north and that he is east of it, the railroad may be fifty or a hundred miles away, while he may be only a mile or two from camp."

The only practical thing I could suggest was this: When a man suddenly discovers that he has lost his bearings and doesn't know which way to go to reach camp or familiar ground, he should above all things avoid getting excited and "losing his head." It is not at all a serious matter and if he will keep cool and use judgment he will come out all right. First let him note carefully his surroundings so he will know the place when he sees it again. Then he can set out in what seems to be the most probable direction to familiar ground, but he must travel in a straight line by the method I described in the last chapter. After traveling a reasonable distance, if no familiar ground is reached he should return to the starting point and try another direction. If all this fails, the various points of the compass having been tried, he should come back to the starting point and camp there until his friends find him. I am presuming that he has lost his bearings under the conditions named by my friend and that he has companions some where not many miles distant. The campfire may help his friends find him and if he fires his gun it may also do some good. It is a very good plan to agree on some sort of a signal to use in case some member of the party loses his way but I know this is seldom done, for nobody cares to let his friends know that he feels the remotest possibility of getting lost. I never leave camp without having with me a good quantity of matches. I always carry a light ax and if the weather is cold I put a blanket in my packsack. Thus, if anything happens to prevent my getting back to camp I am reasonably outfitted for camping out a night.

In my talk about travel by compass I have spoken of keeping direction by the sun and thus doing away to a great extent with frequent reference to the compass. Doubtless the reader has been wondering what he should do on days when the sun is invisible. Fortunately there are few such days unless it is during a rain when of course very little traveling is done. But there are days when fog or clouds obscure the sun for hours and then travel is slow because one must make frequent reference to the compass. The only safe way is to select some conspicuous object in the line of travel each time a compass bearing is taken and to take a new bearing when this object is reached. A dense fog is the worst possible condition for then not only is the sun invisible but one cannot see far enough to choose objective points. I seldom attempt to travel under such conditions but when I do, if I make a half or three-quarters of a mile an hour, providing I have no stream, lake shore or trail to follow, I consider that I am getting along very well. Blinding rain or snow storms also make travel very difficult. I have traveled in a heavy snowstorm by making use of the wind as a guide, in conjunction with the compass. The wind seldom changes during a steady rain or snow storm, and anyway the compass would apprise the wayfarer of a change in the wind before he had gone far out of his course.

There are ways of learning the directions without a compass which may be used in case of emergency. First there is the sun.

South

Sun

THE WATCH AS A COMPASS.

In theory it rises in the east and sets in the west; but in reality it only behaves so on or very near the equator. As we are in the northern hemisphere the sun is of course south of the east and west line all the time, and in winter it is farther south than in summer, because the earth wabbles back and forth throughout the seasons and the northern portion leans away from the path of the sun in winter. As a consequence the sun rises somewhat south of the east in summer and sets a little south of west. In winter it rises still farther south and its path across the sky is always to the south of us. At noon it is straight south. Thus it will be seen that if one knows approximately the time of day he can easily figure out the compass points. Directions by the sun can be learned with much greater accuracy if one has a watch, for knowing the time of day exactly he should know just how far the sun is from the zenith at that time and thus easily locate the true south. Having found it he has but to face in that direction and the north will then be behind him, the east on his left and the west on his right side.

But there is a much better way of getting the compass directions by means of a watch and it is done in this way. Holding the watch so that the hour hand points to a line perpendicular to the sun, count half way from this hour to twelve and this will be south; in other words half way between the hour hand and the figure twelve is south. Count forward from the hour hand to twelve in the forenoon, but in the afternoon the south is half way between the hour hand and twelve, counting back towards twelve. While I may not have made my point clear I believe that the drawing will convey the idea more distinctly. The time shown is 8 p. m. and with the hour hand pointed towards the sun, south would be midway between 8 and 12 or in line with the figure 10.

When the sun is invisible and no compass or other ordinary means of locating directions is available it is advisable to stay in camp if possible. But it is well to know means of finding directions under such conditions for one never knows what may happen and a little knowledge along this line can do no harm even if it is never used. We sometimes read or hear from woodsmen of such means and usually they are given as safe and reliable methods. But they should never be taken too seriously. For instance we are told that moss grows only on the north side of trees, while the larger branches are on the south side. This is true in a general way but conditions have their effect and the shelter of the other trees or nearby hills may reverse the order more or less. But the fact that the sun's rays never directly reach the north side of a tree encourages the growth of moss on that side, while the almost constant sunshine by day, on the south side, causes the sap to flow there more vigorously and thus gives a greater growth to the branches on the south side. In prairie country the prevailing wind, usually from the north, will give a permanent incline to the grass, which may help one to locate directions.

It is seldom necessary to travel at night unless in the north when the snow is soft during the day and travel is better at night. But then the traveler usually has a snowshoe trail to follow or he will have some other way of keeping his directions. If not he can travel by the north star in the same way that he keeps his bearings by the sun during the day. The difference is that the north star does not move across the sky as does the sun, and it is always in the north. To find this star first locate the group which constitute what is commonly known as the dipper. The two stars forming the side of the bowl farthest from the handle are in line with the north star and it is above the open side or top of the dipper bowl.

I have remarked that a man traveling without guidance of any kind always moves in a circle and I think the readers are

★ North Star

★   ★   ★
★   ★   ★

Dipper

★   ★
★   ★

THE STAR THAT MARKS THE TRUE NORTH.

all well acquainted with this fact. I don't know why we do so, but one theory is that one leg is longer than the other and naturally takes a longer step. Others think the trouble is caused by one leg being stronger than the other. But whatever the cause it is a fact that a man wandering aimlessly in the woods will in a short time cross his own trail. This fact was never brought home to me so forcibly as one time when I tried to travel without a compass on a cloudy day. It was early spring and I was traveling on snowshoes, so there was no danger of getting lost, for I had my trail to follow back to camp. I was trying to travel south and was setting a line of traps. I had traveled quite a distance straight south as I supposed when I saw before me a fresh snowshoe trail. I thought at once that some Indian trapper must have invaded my trapping ground. I stepped into the trail and was surprised to find that my snowshoes fitted perfectly into the tracks; then the truth dawned upon me—I had been traveling in a circle. Feeling very foolish I started forward again, resolved to keep a straight course. I found the place where I had made the first turn to the right and here I left the trail and started south again. After traveling perhaps a half mile I again saw a fresh trail ahead and knew at once that I had made another circle. Once more I attempted to strike a straight course south and I traveled the remainder of the way without completing a circle. When the time came to return to camp I had just one trap left and I set it at the end of the trail in a ravine which led down from a hillside. A few days later when I went to look at the traps I climbed to the top of the hill where I had set the last trap, a distance of about 100 yards, and was very much surprised to see below me the lake on which my camp was situated, and the cabin itself not more than a mile away.

To travel straight by that questionable sense known as instinct is absolutely impossible, notwithstanding the stories we hear of Indians, foresters and others who habitually travel this way. Instinct is a very unreliable guide and something more tangible is needed. So when you hear stories of a man who can go anywhere and find his way without failure from one part of the woods to another, it may be wise to pretend credulity, but you may be sure that the story teller is either elaborating or his hero has a very thorough knowledge of the woods and a very reliable, altogether scientific method of keeping his bearings.

The surest way to get lost is to try to travel on strange ground without any guidance whatever, and this is perhaps most easily accomplished by letting some other person lead the way until you have completely lost your bearings. It is a strange fact that few people pay any attention to where they are going if somebody else leads the way and this probably results in more cases of people losing their bearings than all other things combined. I have lost all sense of direction in a very short time by letting some other person lead the way, and this in a farming community. Another easy way to get lost is to follow a game trail, for in such cases the trail and the probability of sighting the game so interests and completely fill one's thoughts that he seldom gives any thought to directions or distance traveled.

To sum up the whole matter of bush travel, one thing stands out as being of the utmost importance and that is to keep the compass points constantly in mind and at the same time have familiar ground from which to start operations. With these two essentials there will be no worry about getting lost to mar one's pleasure and he can travel anywhere he chooses in the big woods.

PACKING

The outfit needed for packing camp equipment is, for each horse, a pack saddle, woolen blankets, pack cinch, 35 or 40 feet of one-half inch manilla rope, another rope of the same size, 20 feet long, a pair of alforjas, a pair of hobbles, and a bell to put on the horse when it is turned out for the night.

A pack saddle consists of two crosses of hardwood, fastened to two flat, round-end pieces of wood, and to this is attached breeching, breast straps and one or two cinches, with the other necessary strap work.

A good pack saddle is strong and well made, of good materials. The leather is a peculiar kind that will not tighten when tied into knots, for the cinch adjustments are usually tied instead of fastened with buckles. When selecting a pack saddle be sure that the breeching and breast straps are long enough for any horse on which the saddle may be used, for the makers frequently try to economize by skimping the rigging, so that they may sell at a lower price.

Be sure also that the saddle fits the horse reasonably well, or it will cause trouble. Most of the pack horses used in the mountains are more or less hollow backed, and the saddle base should not be too long or it will rest on the ends only. On the other hand, if too short it will not be so stable and will also hurt the horse. The double cinch saddle, such as shown in the illustration, is by far the best.

Alforjas are sacks to hang on the sides of the saddle, in which to place all of the small articles of the outfit. They are made of very heavy duck, leather bound, and have straps or loops of rope with which to suspend them from the saddle forks. The proper size is about 24 inches wide, 18 inches high, and when opened out, nine inches deep.

When packing an outfit the horse should be tied and the blanket should be folded and placed on the horse's back. It should not be less than four folds thick and should extend a little ahead and a little behind the saddle base. It must also come down far enough on the sides to form a pad for the alforjas and keep them from rubbing and chafing the animal.

The saddle should then be placed on the folded blanket. Now, at this point, if you want to be kind to the poor horse, grasp the blanket between the two pieces of the saddle base and pull it up a little, so that it is loose over the horse's back. This will allow the saddle to settle down under the weight of the pack and not bind, which it is sure to do if the blanket is not loosened a little as advised. Then both cinches should be tightened, and the breeching and breast straps properly adjusted.

The alforjas are then filled with the small articles of the camp equipment and hung on the forks of the saddle. If the packer is at all conscientious, as he should be, he will see that each sack is of the same weight and that there are no hard or sharp objects so placed that they will injure the animal. Articles which are too big to go into the sacks are then placed on top, where they will rest firmly and not hurt the horse, and the blankets and tent are folded and spread over the top of saddle and alforjas.

At this stage commences what is generally considered the trick of packing, tying the pack to the horse. There are many forms of pack hitch in use and any of them may be learned quite easily by an observing person, nevertheless tying a pack properly can scarcely be done at the first attempt. The most popular of

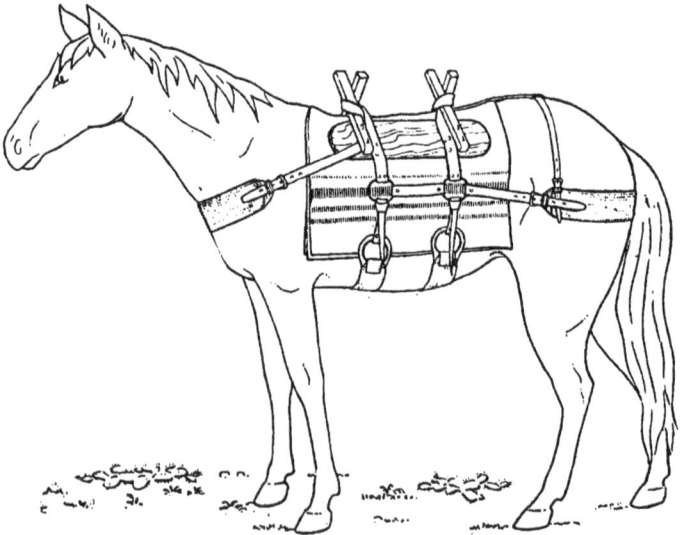

DOUBLE CINCH PACK SADDLE.

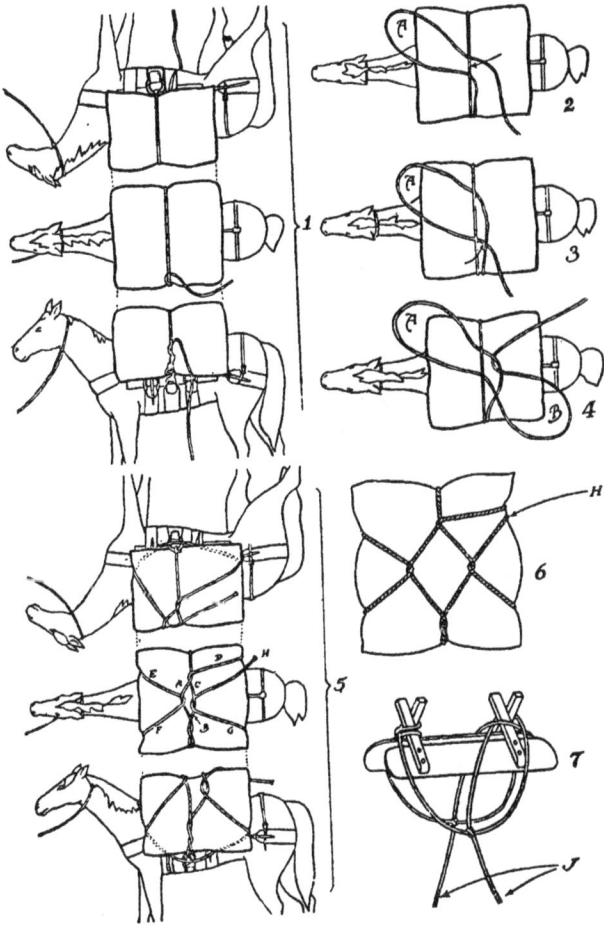

pack ties is what is known as the diamond hitch and all things considered it is probably the best on the list.

To throw the diamond hitch, proceed as follows: Having tied one end of the long rope to the ring of the pack cinch, go to

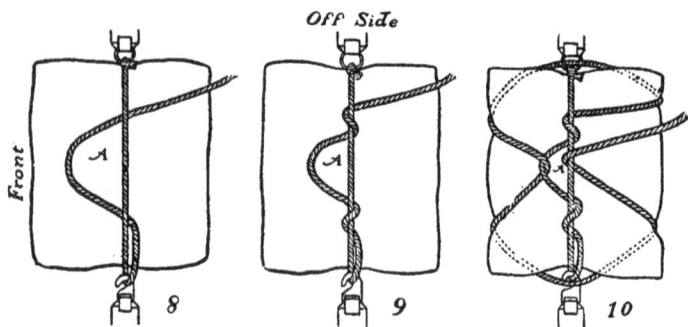

the near side (left) of the horse and throw the cinch over the
pack and horse, then reach under the horse and pick up the
cinch. The hooked end of the cinch is now toward you. Draw
back on the rope until you have all of the slack and pull the rope
down on the near side to the hook of the cinch; double it here
and give it a twist, as shown in Fig. 1, then hook the loop to the
cinch. Now double the free portion of the rope and shove it
through under the part marked by the arrow, from the back,
forming loop A, as shown in Fig. 2. Now give this loop a twist
as shown in Fig. 3, to bring the free portion of the rope down
farther towards the near side. Next grasp this rope at the place
marked by the arrow in Fig. 3, and draw up a part of the free
rope forming loop B, as shown in Fig. 4. All of this time you
have been keeping the rope that crosses the pack fairly tight.
You now go to the off side and pull loop A down over and
under the pack, then come back and put loop B under the pack
on the near side. This will leave the hitch as in Fig. 5 and it is
ready for tightening. Commence first by pulling the rope at
A, then at B, C, D, E, F, G and H, successively. The end of the
rope H is then tied to the ring in the pack cinch at the off side,
and the diamond hitch is completed. The ropes should all be
quite tight, and if they grow loose after awhile they should be
tightened again.

There is another very simple way of tying a diamond hitch,
which though not quite like the one described in detail, is the
same in principle. It is shown very plainly in the three diagrams
reproduced here. As in the first method the rope and cinch are
thrown across the pack to the off side and the cinch is picked up

from beneath the horse, then the rope is drawn up and hooked to the cinch, but the little twist is not put in the rope as in the first method. The free portion of the rope is then thrown across the pack to the off side so that it is parallel with and behind the first rope. Then double this rope on the top of the pack and push it under the first rope from the rear, as shown in Fig. 8. Now bring this loop back over and push it through again, as in Fig. 9, forming the small loop A. Now take the free end of the rope down under the pack on the near side, back and up at the rear, through the loop A again. This is illustrated in Fig. 10. The free end of the rope then goes down under the pack from the rear on the off side and fastens to the cinch ring. The rope is tightened the same as in the other method. This hitch is as good as the other and is more easily remembered, although not as easily tied as the one first described.

Either of these pack ties may be managed easily by one man, but they are tied more rapidly by two men, one standing on the off side and the other on the near side, so that neither need walk around the horse. Then there is the additional advantage in that the rope may be drawn up tight and there is no danger that it will slip, as one or the other of the men can be holding the rope all the time the pack is being tied.

In addition to the pack ties described there is another hitch that should be learned as it is useful for securing packages to the pack saddle when alforjas are not used, also for holding packs to the sides of the saddle while tying the diamond hitch. There are several methods of fixing a sling rope and the mode I am going to describe is illustrated in Fig. 7.

For this purpose the shorter length of rope is brought into use. It is doubled in the middle and looped around the front forks of the pack saddle, then one-half of the rope is taken to the near side and the other is dropped on the off side. Taking either half of the rope, you allow sufficient slack to hold the pack at the proper height then bring the rope around the rear forks, then down to the centre of the slack portion, where it is tied. The pack is then fixed in this loop and the other side is arranged the same way. After both packs are properly slung the ends of the rope are brought up on top and tied together.

There are many forms of pack hitches other than those described, although the diamond hitch is most used and more popular than any of the others.

A pack horse should never be overloaded, and the animal cannot carry as great a load as many people expect. Two hundred pounds is the limit for any pack, and 150 is a more reasonable load. For long journeys the pack, per horse, should not weigh this much. A hundred or a 125 is all that should be allotted to any animal.

A pack train may consist of any number of pack animals, and if there are enough riders in the party one man rides between each two pack horses. I mean by that, one rider goes ahead leading a horse behind him. That horse is followed by another rider, then another pack horse, etc. If there are not enough men in the party for this, two pack animals are placed between two riders. The men may lead the horses if they are inclined to wander from the route, but ordinarily this is not necessary, as the animals will keep in line. But if you lead a pack horse do not grow tired of holding the rope and tie it to the horn of the saddle. This is a dangerous practice and may result in serious injury to the one who is so thoughtless, for the pack horse may become frightened and bolt or may swing around, wrapping the rope around the rider.

Pack horses are always more or less troublesome, and the man who uses them should have a bountiful supply of patience. At night the animals are hobbled, which means that their front feet are fastened together with hobbles, so that they cannot travel fast or far. Too much dependence should not be placed on these retarders, for Western horses soon learn to travel quite rapidly when thus impeded, and will sometimes set out for home while the master sleeps. A good practice is to picket one or two horses in the best spots of pasture to be found, and hobble the remaining animals. They are not so likely to leave if this is done, and if they do, the picketed horses must remain behind, which insures at least a mount with which to follow the runaways. Also put a bell on each horse, as this will aid in locating the animals in the morning.

Horse feed cannot be carried, and Western horses seldom get any food except what they can find at night or while they are not in use, and on the plains or in the mountains where vegetation is scanty they sometimes do not get as much as they require. Under such circumstances they should not be loaded too heavily, or traveled too far in a day, and it may even be necessary, on a long journey to take an occasional day of rest to allow the horses to recuperate.

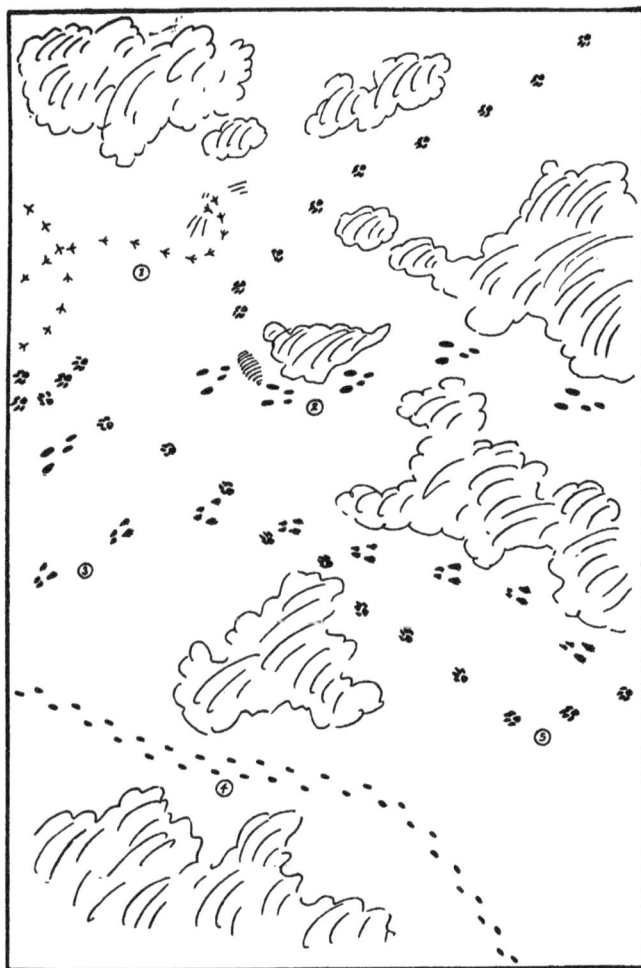

ANIMAL TRACKS. 1, PARTRIDGE; 2, RABBIT; 3, SQUIRREL; 4, SKUNK; AND 5, A FEW FOX TRACKS.

www.ingramcontent.com/pod-product-compliance
Lightning Source LLC
Chambersburg PA
CBHW021533260326
41914CB00001B/5